Instructor's Resource Manual

Diane Moczar
Northern Virginia Community College

SOURCES OF THE WESTERN TRADITION

Third Edition

Volumes I and II

Marvin Perry
Baruch College, City University of New York

Joseph R. Peden
Baruch College, City University of New York

Theodore H. Von Laue
Clark University

George Bock, *Editorial Associate*

Houghton Mifflin Company Boston Toronto
Geneva, IL Palo Alto Princeton, NJ

Copyright © 1995 by Houghton Mifflin Company.
All rights reserved.

Permission is hereby granted to teachers to reprint or photocopy in classroom quantities the pages or sheets in this work that carry a Houghton Mifflin Company copyright notice. These pages are designed to be reproduced by teachers for use in their classes with accompanying Houghton Mifflin material, provided each copy made shows the copyright notice. Such copies may not be sold and further distribution is expressly prohibited. Except as authorized above, prior written permission must be obtained from Houghton Mifflin Company to reproduce or transmit this work or portions thererof in any other form or by any other electronic or mechanical means, including any information storage or retrieval system, unless expressly permitted by federal copyright law. Address inquiries to College Permissions, Houghton Mifflin Company, 222 Berkeley Street, Boston, MA 02116.

Printed in the U.S.A.

ISBN: 0-395-57309-2

123456789-VG-98 97 96 95 94

CONTENTS

PREFACE

Through reading the selections in this volume, students will gain an understanding and appreciation of the foundations of Western civilization. The various strands from which the culture of the West is woven are represented, of which the most significant in Volume I are the intellectual achievements of Greece and the Judeo-Christian religious tradition. These two elements met in the culture of the late Roman Empire, survived the Dark Ages, and were harmonized during the Middle Ages into a new and dynamic cultural synthesis—the civilization of Christendom.

While most of the readings in Volume I are concerned with the rise and development of this new European civilization, the later chapters deal with movements that would lead to the destruction of the old synthesis and the emergence of the modern world. Thus the intellectual, spiritual, and political ferment of the Renaissance, Reformation and Enlightenment periods are explained in the final chapters of Volume I.

The readings in Volume II have a dual focus: the unraveling of the intellectual, spiritual, and cultural synthesis that underlay the civilization of Christendom, and the hammering out of a new mental framework for what we call the modern world. In order for students to appreciate the great novelty of the ideas expressed in many of the selections in the first part of this volume, they will need some familiarity with the thought and culture of premodern Europe. The Introduction to Volume II is therefore extremely important as a summary of earlier thought and its radical contrast with the modern mentality.

Although students will find many of the readings immediately appealing—particularly those found in the latter part of the book that deal with contemporary issues—they may find some of the earlier samples of Humanist and Enlightenment thought rather heavy going. Although the relevance of some of these selections will become apparent only in the light of subsequent history, they are crucial for understanding the development of the modern world. They therefore repay the extra effort their comprehension may require of both instructor and students.

It might be emphasized by the instructor that the readings given here represent only a small sampling of the vast output of our civilization. If students can be induced to read more of what they will merely taste in *Sources of the Western Tradition,* that tradition will be well served.

D.M.

INTRODUCTION

WHY ORIGINAL SOURCES?

"I never use original sources," said a colleague. "They're not interesting enough." "Too difficult for our students," warned the chairman of a community college history department. "Only for honors classes," stated another instructor.

Students, however, disagreed. An informal survey of nearly one hundred community college students in three different nonhonors Western Civilization classes, who had used one or the other of the volumes of *Sources of the Western Tradition*, showed virtually unanimous enthusiasm for reading original texts. In anonymous (and voluntary) comments, the students expressed their fascination with the immediate contact with the past provided by the readings in *Sources*. They stressed both the attraction of eyewitness accounts and the satisfaction of reading for oneself what a great thinker had to say, rather than relying on a secondary account of what was said. A number of students confessed to reading the book for pure pleasure: "Your money is not wasted because you can also read it for pleasure," wrote one, while another stated "I ... would recommend it to someone even if they weren't enrolled in a history class."

What accounts for the discrepancy in viewpoint between professors and students on the use of original texts in teaching history? There are any number of possible explanations. Instructors who were not exposed to the use of

Copyright © 1995 Houghton Mifflin Company. All rights reserved.

sources in their undergraduate training are often reluctant to start using an unfamiliar resource. Some have an impression that the great works of the past are somehow "difficult," or too remote from contemporary life to be of interest to their classes.

Possibly the greatest deterrent to incorporating sources into teaching, however, is that their effectiveness depends on a somewhat different approach from the lecture method, and many instructors are not sure how to modify their classroom style. After a few failed attempts to promote class discussion of a reading, professors understandably revert to the lecture format and abandon the study of sources. The following suggestions may be of help to the instructor who wants to introduce students to the exhilarating experience of direct contact with the "raw material" of history. Implicit in this approach is the premise that the writers are expressing concepts that a modern reader can grasp. There is no deconstructionism here, no queries such as: "How do we know the writer means what he says?" "What would he say if he meant something entirely different?" "What would the text say if we replaced its surface meaning with our own assumptions about the underlying assumptions of the author?" With that proviso, here are the suggestions.

Sources as Adjunct Material

The most common use of source collections like *Sources of the Western Tradition* is to supplement classroom lectures and standard textbooks. For this purpose, the material may be used in several ways, of which four are discussed below:

Copyright © 1995 Houghton Mifflin Company. All rights reserved.

1. Homework Assignments

Students may be assigned one or more readings that relate to the topics currently being studied in class. The assignment might consist of either (a) answering, in writing, some or all of the questions at the end of the selections, or (b) writing a short essay reacting to the reading—does the student agree or disagree with the ideas expressed and why?

2. Extra-Credit Work

Students may be given a choice of readings on which to comment in writing, either by answering questions or writing an essay.

3. Term Papers

Some chapters are suitable for use as the core of a term paper or other substantial project. The chapters on the French and Russian revolutions in Volume II are excellent examples of groups of readings that could be utilized in this way. Many other chapters in both volumes could also be so utilized. The student would combine outside research on a given topic with a study of the primary material found in *Sources,* using the readings to illustrate conclusions drawn from research.

4. Class Discussion

The attempt to use source material to stimulate class discussion is often what sours instructors on the whole idea of assigning readings. The students won't discuss, complains the instructor; they sit there, completely unmoved by any stimulating questions the professor may pose. It is true that classroom discussion is not always a success; in very large classes it is obviously inappropriate, but even in quite

Copyright © 1995 Houghton Mifflin Company. All rights reserved.

small groups there is often student resistance to the idea. As one student wrote in an anonymous midterm evaluation, "I like it that you don't make us talk when we don't want to." Often, however, evoking a good discussion is largely a matter of technique. It is a rare group of students that cannot be moved to speech after reading a text such as the Volume I selection by Cato on women's rights (or lack thereof). The instructor must give some thought to type of questions that will best stimulate response (see suggestions for each chapter in this *Manual*), but may also use such devices as arguing in favor of an outrageous opinion. (Defending Cato, for example, invariably arouses discussion.) Also remember that a classroom discussion is not necessarily a failure because not all students participate; students can learn from listening to discussions. This observation raises the question of whether classroom participation should be graded. Many professors who make frequent use of the discussion method have abandoned the grading of participation because of the obvious danger of penalizing mere shyness or rewarding natural loquaciousness. Other instructors still think that grading prompts discussion.

Sources as Primary Instructional Material

Some teachers structure an intellectual history course around *Sources of the Western Tradition* as the only text or combined with outside readings. Some colleges offer an intensive one-semester course in European intellectual history that requires the use of both volumes of *Sources*. A course of this type works best with small classes and a seminar approach; this means teaching largely through discussion, with a minimum of lecturing. The advantage of this

 Copyright © 1995 Houghton Mifflin Company. All rights reserved.

type of course is that far more of the book can be used than in courses where it is read only as an addition to a (usually very large) textbook. Since discussion plays a more essential role in a seminar course, the instructor might wish to read some of the excellent material published by the Great Books Foundation about leading discussions on primary texts.

All too often in the mind of the student, history is a jumble of opinions and interpretations read in a textbook or heard in a lecture. Although lectures and textbooks are indispensable, there is also much to be said for "letting the past speak for itself" to the student, through primary sources. To read eyewitness accounts of great events in history, from the destruction of Carthage by the Romans to famine engineered by Stalin in the Ukraine, is to see history happening in one's imagination. To follow Descartes's account of how he arrived at his famous philosophical principle is to follow his road for oneself, not to be told about it by someone else. This "firsthand" seeing and knowing imparts a self-confidence and discernment to the learner that is one of the benefits of education. We hope the summaries and suggestions in this manual will aid the instructor to make the seeing and the knowing easier and more enjoyable for history students.

Copyright © 1995 Houghton Mifflin Company. All rights reserved.

CHAPTER 1

THE NEAR EAST

Overview of the Chapter

The importance of the ancient Near Eastern cultures to Western civilization is brought out in the introduction to the chapter. The societies that developed around the eastern Mediterranean were unlike those in some other parts of the world that tended to deny the importance (or even the reality) of material things and thus produced static, ethereal, inward-turning cultures—Harappa in ancient India is an example. The Near Eastern peoples, on the contrary, although they were preoccupied with religion and ritual, produced cultures characterized by the creative use of material things, technical innovations, law, literature, and efficient government.

Section 1. Mesopotamian Protest Against Death

The *Epic of Gilgamesh* is a poignant, probing example of the quest of the human mind for immortality and for the answers to the ultimate questions posed by human existence.

In the form of an epic tale, the story of Gilgamesh touches on many themes, such as the power and capriciousness of the Mesopotamian gods, the nature of friendship, and especially, the problem of death.

Copyright © 1995 Houghton Mifflin Company. All rights reserved.

Section 2. Mesopotamian Concepts of Justice

Law codes are a valuable source of information for the historian. The laws of many ancient peoples reflect their basic attitudes, which are often surprisingly similar to those of much later times.

The excerpts from Hammurabi's famous *Code* reveal much about Babylonian society as well as about the king's concept of how order and justice should be maintained in his state. Even consumer rights and physicians' malpractice are provided for. In an early example of social welfare legislation, doctors' fees are adjusted according to the patient's ability to pay.

Section 3. Divine Kingship

The concept of political authority as having a divine origin was common to nearly all peoples and ages until modern times. Human beings, it was thought, were not the source of their own existence; hence, any authority an individual might wield over others could not be derived from himself, but from the god who created him.

Hymns to the Pharaohs reflects the view of the Egyptian ruler as a divine intermediary through whom blessings came to the people, and as one who would experience immortality after death.

Guidelines for the Ruler outlines the ethical principles and political ideals according to which the pharaohs were to carry out their responsibilities.

Copyright © 1995 Houghton Mifflin Company. All rights reserved.

Section 4. Religious Inspiration of Akhenaten

Most Near Eastern religions posited the existence of many gods. Apart from the Hebrews, discussed in Chapter 2, only the pharaoh Akhenaten, a remarkable figure in many ways, seems to have developed a religion honoring only one god.

The *Hymn to Aton* expresses the pharaoh's idea of the sun god as an all-powerful and beneficent creator. The one god of Akhenaten is intimately involved with the world and especially protective of the people of Egypt.

Section 5. Empire Builders

The readings included in this section come from two of the many empires that rose and fell in the ancient Near East, all of them based on conquest, effective governmental organization, and often harsh rule. *Inscription of Tiglath Pileser I* depicts the legendary ruthlessness and energy of the Assyrian kings, as well as something of their mentality. In the excerpts from ancient texts, the renowned rulers Cyrus and Darius describe some of their achievements.

Section 6. The Myth-making Outlook of the Ancient Near East

As the introduction to this section states, the ancient Near Eastern mentality differed from the modern scientific mentality in a number of ways. Ancient thinkers used their intellects to probe the secrets of the universe, but unlike modern scientists who ask *how* things happen and are satisfied with knowing which natural laws are operating, the ancients were often exclusively interested in final causality—the ultimate reason *why* things occurred in the first place. Although they did observe and make use of the workings of nature in such areas as

Copyright © 1995 Houghton Mifflin Company. All rights reserved.

astronomy and flood prediction, the thinkers of the Near East were more concerned with divine intervention in the world of nature. The welter of theological explanations, many of which reflect themes common to a number of neighboring social groups, was expressed in poetic and mythical form.

Personification of Natural Objects shows the tendency of the mythic approach to attribute human or divine qualities to things. It is not completely clear how much of what is expressed in these segments was taken literally and how much was merely poetic symbolism.

Enuma elish is an example of a creation myth. Unlike the Hebrew account of the creation of the world from nothing, the Babylonian version deals with the organization of the world by a god from preexisting matter.

Lament for Ur attributes a disaster that struck the famous city to divine displeasure. The reading may refer to the starvation and destruction of Ur by Elamites and Amorites in the third millennium B.C.

Questions for Discussion or Essay Assignments

1. Does anything in the anxiety and disillusion of Gilgamesh have a parallel in today's society, or is the theme of the tale irrelevant to the modern world?

2. Make a list of the areas in which Hammurabi's law code can furnish information about Babylonian society; consider technical skills, family life, attitude toward private property, and so on. How might Hammurabi have defined *justice*?

Copyright © 1995 Houghton Mifflin Company. All rights reserved.

3. Note the attributes of the god of Akhenaten in order to compare them later with other conceptions of the supreme divinity that appear in later chapters.

4. Compare the selections from Assyrian and Persian rulers. Are there any types of accomplishments of which they are all proud? What similarities and differences do you find in all three texts?

5. If the people of Ur had understood the natural causes a work in the destruction of their city, do you think it would have satisfied their desire to know why it happened, or would they say that the gods had simply made use of circumstances that they themselves controlled?

Multiple Choice Questions

1. The mood of the tale of Gilgamesh may be termed
   a. carefree.
   b. tragic.
   c. cheerful.
   d. humorous.

2. Gilgamesh finds the ultimate answer to the problem of death
   a. in Siduri's advice to enjoy life
   b. in love.
   c. nowhere.
   d. in materialism.

3. In ancient Babylonia, a criminal was likely to receive
   a. a fine or loss of life or limb.
   b. parole.
   c. a warning.
   d. imprisonment.

Copyright © 1995 Houghton Mifflin Company. All rights reserved.

4. Hammurabi's *Code* provided for different penalties according to
   a. social class.
   b. motive.
   c. age.
   d. the whim of the judge.

5. Babylonian law supported
   a. the indissolubility of marriage.
   b. the absolute authority of the husband.
   c. complete equality of men and women.
   d. some legal rights for women and children.

6. The Egyptian pharaohs were looked upon as
   a. democratic leaders.
   b. evil despots.
   c. god-given divine rulers.
   d. irrelevant to Egyptian life.

7. The hymn to Pharaoh Rameses IV expresses the concept of the Egyptian ruler as the source of
   a. strict justice.
   b. vengeance.
   c. civil strife.
   d. the well-being of the people.

8. *Guidelines for the Ruler* depicts the desire of the pharaoh to promote
   a. his family's wealth and power.
   b. justice and social welfare.
   c. foreign conquest.
   d. scientific advancement.

9. The *Guidelines* recommend basing civil service on
   a. individual competence.
   b. social rank.
   c. race.
   d. wealth.

Copyright © 1995 Houghton Mifflin Company. All rights reserved.

10. The pharaoh Akhenaten believed in
    a. one benevolent god.
    b. many gods.
    c. no gods.
    d. an evil god.

11. The Assyrians were
    a. a pastoral tribe.
    b. warlike conquerors.
    c. pacifists.
    d. seafarers.

12. Cyrus the Great seemed to place a high value on
    a. money.
    b. atheism.
    c. peace and good adminstration.
    d. brutal conquest.

13. The ancient Mesopotamians often regarded material things as
    a. combinations of atoms.
    b. having no real existence.
    c. living.
    d. useless.

14. According to *Enuma elish,* Marduk made human beings
    a. out of benevolence.
    b. as food for the animals.
    c. out of malice.
    d. to serve the gods.

15. *Lament for Ur* is probably intended as
    a. an allegory.
    b. fiction.
    c. a poetic account of a real event.
    d. a flood myth.

 Copyright © 1995 Houghton Mifflin Company. All rights reserved.

Multiple Choice Answers

1.	b	6.	c	11.	b
2.	c	7.	d	12.	c
3.	a	8.	b	13.	c
4.	a	9.	a	14.	d
5.	d	10.	a	15.	c

Copyright © 1995 Houghton Mifflin Company. All rights reserved.

CHAPTER 2

THE HEBREWS

Overview of the Chapter

The overwhelming significance of Hebrew thought for Western civilization can hardly be exaggerated. The ideas of one transcendent God, a theological moral code, and great dignity accorded to human beings are some of the many points on which Hebrew thought differed radically from that of their contemporaries. Furthermore, much of the Hebrew world-view is expressed in language of striking poetic beauty that has made the Bible a masterpiece of world literature and a powerful influence on later Western writers in all countries.

Section 1. Hebrew Cosmogony and Anthropology

The texts illustrate the majesty, as well as the profound novelty, of the ideas incorporated into the Bible. The reading from Genesis contains the first three chapters of the Bible. A careful reading will reveal themes of permanent relevance for civilization: the existence and attributes of God, the nature of human beings, the origin of evil.

Section 2. God's Greatness and Human Dignity

The theological outlook that saw creation as good necessarily produced a positive view of nature and of human beings—the highest of earthly creatures, ranking just beneath the

Copyright © 1995 Houghton Mifflin Company. All rights reserved.

pure spirits, angels, which appear elsewhere in the Old Testament.

Psalm 8 extols, in moving poetic language, God's power and kindness and the place in creation of human beings.

Psalm 104 is a beautiful paean to the glory and might of God and his benevolent providence over all creatures.

Section 3. The Covenant and the Ten Commandments

The first reading in the chapter discusses the importance of the covenant between God nd his "chosen people," and the obligations laid on the Hebrews. Section 3 contains readings illustrating these points.

The Covenant in Exodus records God's words and the Hebrews' response, instituting the alliance between God and the Jews.

The *Ten Commandments* in Exodus give the text of the laws received by Moses concerning the obligations of human beings, first to God and then to each other.

Section 4. Humaneness of Hebrew Laws

In its protection of slaves, unwanted children, and the poor, Hebrew legislation was unique in the ancient world. The law derived its authority from having been revealed by God.

The reading from Leviticus illustrates the Hebrews' obligations toward others, including foreigners, and contains the immortal injunction, "You shall love your neighbor as yourself."

The reading from Deuteronomy deals with the establishment of a legal system and elaborates further obligations of justice. In this passage the Jews are frequently reminded of their

Copyright © 1995 Houghton Mifflin Company. All rights reserved.

former miserable state as slaves in Egypt before their deliverance by God.

Section 5. The Age of Classical Prophecy

The moral law is one thing and its practice is another. In the course of their history, the Hebrews sometimes failed to live up to the high standard that God had set for them, and tended to overemphasize ritual practices over moral behavior. The task of the prophets was to remind the Hebrews of God's laws, often scathingly criticizing the people.

The first Isaiah reading is an example of the prophetic denunciation of hypocrisy and injustice.

The reading from Second Isaiah ridicules the practice of making and worshiping idols and shows the absurdity and irrationality of invoking the favor of something a human being has made. The struggle against idolatry would persist into the Christian era, with Roman idol-makers often spearheading persecution of the Christians.

The final reading from Isaiah envisages a time of peace for the human race after its acknowledgment of the one true God and his rule.

Questions for Discussion or Essay Assignments

1. How would Isaiah answer the questions that tormented Gilgamesh (Chapter 1)?

2. How would the Hebrews define *justice*, and how would their definition differ from Hammurabi's?

3. What concept of God do you get from the Hebrew texts? Compare this concept with those of (a) Akhenaten's god and (b) the

 Copyright © 1995 Houghton Mifflin Company. All rights reserved.

gods depicted in the *Epic of Gilgamesh* and *Enuma elish*.

4. What idea of human nature is reflected in the Hebrew writings? In what ways does this concept differ from the views of human nature found in the Egyptian and Mesopotamian texts in Chapter 1?

5. How would slaveholders in the American South have reacted to verse 15 of the second reading in Section 4?

Multiple Choice Questions

1. The Hebrews believed in
   a. three gods.
   b. god-kings.
   c. one god.
   d. no gods.

2. For the Hebrews, God's role in history is
   a. active and benevolent.
   b. absent.
   c. active and harsh.
   d. ineffective.

3. The God of Israel is
   a. an impersonal force.
   b. a personal god.
   c. a personification of natural forces.
   d. an idol.

4. To reconcile people with God, God promised to send
   a. prophets.
   b. kings.
   c. priests.
   d. a messiah.

Copyright © 1995 Houghton Mifflin Company. All rights reserved.

5. For the Hebrews, the creation of the world was described in
   a. *Enuma elish*.
   b. the *Epic of Gilgamesh*.
   c. Genesis.
   d. Deuteronomy.

6. According to Genesis, creation is
   a. evil.
   b. partially good, partially evil.
   c. good.
   d. neither good nor bad.

7. The sin of Adam and Eve was one of
   a. ignorance.
   b. disobedience.
   c. passion.
   d. hatred.

8. After the sin of Adam and Eve, God
   a. continued to care for human beings and nature.
   b. abandoned the human race.
   c. destroyed the world.
   d. showed hatred for creation.

9. According to Hebrew theology, a human being's place in the world is that of
   a. one animal among other animals.
   b. a slave to cosmic forces.
   c. a god.
   d. the highest of earthly creatures, but subject to God.

10. The moral basis of Hebrew ethical and legal theory was the
    a. Ten Commandments.
    b. Psalms.
    c. Code of Hammurabi.
    d. laws of Draco.

Copyright © 1995 Houghton Mifflin Company. All rights reserved.

11. Hebrew legal writings dealt with justice among
    a. nations.
    b. property owners.
    c. nobles.
    d. all individuals.

12. The prophets generally
    a. wrote plays.
    b. flattered and praised the Jews.
    c. reminded the people of their transgressions.
    d. studied astronomy.

13. Hebrew texts strongly condemn
    a. idolatry.
    b. slavery.
    c. meat-eating.
    d. warfare.

14. The Jews expected injustice to be
    a. tolerated by God.
    b. eliminated from the earth.
    c. punished by God.
    d. rewarded on earth.

15. Isaiah foretold an era of peace if the nations of the world would
    a. set up the United Nations.
    b. acknowledge the rule of the true God.
    c. renounce warfare.
    d. send representatives to Jerusalem.

Multiple Choice Answers

1.	c	6.	c	11.	d
2.	a	7.	b	12.	c
3.	b	8.	a	13.	a
4.	d	9.	d	14.	c
5.	c	10.	a	15.	b

Copyright © 1995 Houghton Mifflin Company. All rights reserved.

CHAPTER 3

THE GREEKS

Overview of the Chapter

This chapter, like the one on the Hebrews, is of primary importance for an understanding of Western civilization. Although it provides a broad sampling of texts, the astonishing richness of the Greek achievement defies summation. The instructor might want to assign one or more entire works, such as the whole *Iliad* or a Platonic dialogue, such as the *Gorgias, Crito,* or *Phaedo* (which includes the touching scene of Socrates' death).

Section 1. Homer: The Educator of Greece

It would be difficult to overestimate the influence of Homer on Western civilization. Not only were his works the foundation of Greek literature and education, but they have exercised a fascination for all subsequent generations. Homer's stories are unforgettable as literature, and historians and archaeologists continue to search for the reality behind the tale of Troy and the journey of Odysseus.

The Iliad excerpts give a brief glimpse of the power of Homeric language and character depiction, even when translated from its original Greek and changed from poetry to prose.

 Copyright © 1995 Houghton Mifflin Company. All rights reserved.

Section 2. Early Greek Philosophy: The Emancipation of Thought from Myth

The Greeks were the first thinkers to develop principles of systematic intellectual analysis. By means of methodical observation and logical deduction, the early philosophers investigated the behavior and causes of natural things. They did not seek to know only the final, divine cause that had been posited by earlier thinkers to explain natural occurrences, but looked for what they called proximate causes—how things operated.

Aristotle's brief account of the thought of Thales of Miletus shows this Ionian philosopher's attempt to account for the origin of material things.

The reading titled *Anaximander* gives a number of that philosopher's explanations for existing things and living creatures. Although often fantastic to us, these explanations reveal the desire to understand the world in terms of principles other than direct divine intervention.

Aristotle's remarks in *Pythagoras* reveal the early Greek fascination with numbers, which they would pursue both in developing mathematical systems and in a number-oriented mysticism that was to influence later religious thought.

Section 3. The Expansion of Reason

Systematic, rational investigation expanded into most areas of Greek thought and led to further philosophical and scientific developments. The readings in this section show the rational approach in three different disciplines.

Copyright © 1995 Houghton Mifflin Company. All rights reserved.

The excerpts from the writings of Hippocrates show the famous physician's logical analysis of opinions advanced to explain epilepsy.

Thucydides' *Method of Historical Inquiry* illustrates the rational approach to history that insists on careful reporting of facts and evaluation of evidence. In contrast to Herodotus, to whom Thucydides may be referring sarcastically in this passage, the historian of the Peloponnesian War insisted on a critical and factual history devoid of myth and hearsay.

The Sophists were bitterly challenged by Socrates for teaching clever argumentation rather than truth. In *Religion as a Human Invention,* the Sophist Critias gives his theory about how the human belief in deities came about.

Section 4. Greek Art

The pictures in this section illustrate the characteristics of harmony, realism, and rationality of Greek art and architecture as discussed in the text. They also point up differences between the archaic and classical styles, and the influence of Greek artistic principles even in modern times.

Section 5. Humanism

The Greek ideal of civilized man included physical prowess as well as virtue and high achievement in a worthy endeavor. Greek literature frequently gave expression to these ideals.

Pindar's poetic excerpt in *The Pursuit of Excellence* expresses poignantly the glory and, at the same time, the transitory nature of human achievement.

In *The Wonders of Man,* Sophocles praises the attainments of civilized man, as opposed to

 Copyright © 1995 Houghton Mifflin Company. All rights reserved.

"anarchic" man. He also, however, acknowledges the tragic mortality of human beings.

Section 6. Greek Drama

Greek playwrights excelled at both comedy and tragedy, and created masterpieces which are still popular today. This section focuses on tragedy.

The passages from *Antigone* by Sophocles illustrate some of the ideas and scenes that have made this play such a powerful and perennially relevant work of art. During the German occupation of Paris during World War II, Jean Anouilh, a French dramatist, wrote a version of this play in which the audience was able to recognize clearly the parallels with their own situation.

Section 7. Athenian Greatness

The achievements of the city-state of Athens in the fifth century B.C. rival or surpass those of any other age. In government, philosophy, silence, and all the arts, the period was indeed a golden age.

The Funeral Oration of Pericles, recorded by Thucydides, sums up the greatness of Athens. Although Athenian glory cannot be denied, there was, of course, another side to the picture. The Athenian democracy so glowingly described by Pericles was capable of injustice, imperialism, and tyrannical acts; it was also limited to free, male, native-born citizens. Expenditures on public entertainment and civic embellishment unbalanced the budget. Finally, although Pericles praises the Athenians' lack of military training and practice and the lack of protection of their military secrets, it must be also remembered that Athens lost the war.

Copyright © 1995 Houghton Mifflin Company. All rights reserved.

Section 8. The Status of Women in Classical Greek Society

The Greek political and cultural world was inhabited mainly by free male citizens, to the exclusion of slaves, foreigners, and women. Men generally preferred each other's company, and often homosexual relationships, to the society of women. As a result, although women have an honorable place in much of Greek literature, their status in the city-state was not very high.

Xenophon's *Oeconomicus* gives an insight into Greek marriage customs, including the apparently great discrepancy in age between husband and wife. In this passage, marriage is looked upon as a real partnership characterized by affection and honor.

The dramatist Aristophanes wittily portrays, in the comedy *Lysistrata,* a "battle of the sexes," in which the dialogue touches on many of the women's grievances and views of Athenian politics.

Section 9. The Peloponnesian War

Athenian imperial ambitions contributed to the war that pitted the Greek city-states against each other and ended with the defeat of Athens by Sparta. The subsequent decline of Sparta and of other states that attempted to maintain hegemony in Greece led to the end of the great age of Greece.

The excerpts from Thucydides' account of the war show the great historian's gift for analyzing political motives and policies and clarifying complex issues by means of carefully constructed speeches and dialogues.

 Copyright © 1995 Houghton Mifflin Company. All rights reserved.

Section 10. Socrates: The Rational Individual

Socrates was one of the greatest of all Western philosophers. Unlike many of his predecessors, he was uninterested in the study of nature or the art of persuasive argument. His concern was to stimulate self-knowledge in his pupils and to lead them to discover for themselves, through active participation in disciplined discussion, what they could know (and also what they did not know) and how the morally good man should live.

The Apology, from Plato's account of Socrates' speech at his trial, illuminates both the character of the philosopher and the issues at stake in his trial.

Section 11. Plato: The Philosopher-King

Like his master, Plato was concerned with ethics and the morally good life, both for the individual and for society. His application of Socratic principles led him to develop a philosophy that dealt with many of the great questions that have concerned Western thinkers ever since. A major theme elaborated by Plato was the nature of the state and the just society.

The Republic excerpts give some of Plato's political views, including his famous defense of the philosopher-king, and the celebrated "cave" passage.

Section 12. Aristotle: Science and Politics

Although a pupil of Plato, Aristotle developed a philosophy that differed considerably from that of his teacher. The scope of Aristotle's interests was enormous. Natural science, logic, ethics, politics, esthetics, psychology, and metaphysics were some of the areas to which he

Copyright © 1995 Houghton Mifflin Company. All rights reserved.

applied methods and categories of systematic investigation that were often his best invention. It has been said that everyone is born either a Platonist or an Aristotelian; certainly these two towering figures have influenced Western thought up to the present time.

The excerpts from *History of Animals* and *Politics* show several facets of Aristotle's approach, such as his careful observation and collection of data and his method of drawing conclusions from established premises.

Section 13. Alexander the Great and the Hellenistic World

Aristotle's Macedonian pupil Alexander became a legend in his own time, and for over two thousand years, countless poems, plays, novels, films, and historical studies about him testify to a fascination with the great conqueror who died so young. The cultural unity he brought to the vast territory he conquered facilitated in later eras both the eastern conquests of Rome and the spread of the new doctrine of Christianity.

The Fortune of Alexander by Plutarch—written hundreds of years after Alexander's death—attributes to the king the noble plan of bringing unity, justice, and Greek civilization to his multiracial empire.

Section 14. Hellenistic Philosophy: Epicureanism

The Hellenistic period, though not the equal of the golden age of Athens in intellectual achievement, was still a time of progress in such areas as art, mathematics, science, and some types of literature. In philosophy, the ideal of the withdrawal of the individual from involvement in society for the purpose of

 Copyright © 1995 Houghton Mifflin Company. All rights reserved.

pursuing his own happiness emerged in various forms.

The Prudent Pursuit of Pleasure contains some of the principles elaborated by the Hellenistic philosopher Epicurus. Neither fulfillment of religious duty nor service to the common good was the goal of the Epicurean, but a simple life of well-ordered pleasure and noninvolvement in the world.

Section 15. *Hellenization:* The Impact of Greek Culture on the Jews

The spread of Greek civilization and lifestyle under Alexander and his successors provoked varying degrees of cultural disorientation and tension throughout the Hellenistic world. The inevitable clash between Greek and Jewish values became open violence with the attempts of Antiochus IV to force Hellenization on the Jews.

The *First Book of Maccabees* describes the cruelty of Antiochus and the heroic resistance of the Jews who remained faithful to their religion.

The selection from *Philo of Alexandria* illustrates the principle that true faith and true reason cannot contradict each other since God is the author of both. In his appreciation of Greek philosophy and use of its methods to explore theological questions, Philo was a forerunner of Christian medieval thinkers who were both philosophers and theologians.

Questions for Discussion or Essay Assignments

1. Compare the tragic view of life expressed by Pindar in Section 5 with that of Gilgamesh in Chapter 1. Are there any differences? Would the Hebrew psalmist (Chapter 2) agree with them?

Copyright © 1995 Houghton Mifflin Company. All rights reserved.

2. Does Critias (Section 3) think that the state of man before the laws were devised was preferable to the rule of the "dictator" Justice, and its slave "arrogance"? Does his account of the invention of religion resemble myth or logical demonstration?

3. In contrast to some Eastern cultures, which tended to negate or spiritualize the material world, the Greeks considered the material world as real, good, and worthy of rational investigation. Which readings best illustrate this emphasis on the use of the intellect in analyzing reality?

4. Would you call Aristotle's *History of Animals* a scientific work? Why or why not?

5. Would you like to read more from the works of authors who appear in this chapter? If so, list the authors and explain why they interest you.

Multiple Choice Questions

1. Homer's works may be said to reflect the ideals of
   a. a peaceful nation.
   b. a warrior society.
   c. inhuman barbarians.
   d. a group of philosophers.

2. For the Greeks, the material world was
   a. an illusion.
   b. real and comprehensible.
   c. evil.
   d. useless.

Copyright © 1995 Houghton Mifflin Company. All rights reserved.

3. Early Greek philosophers were interested in
   a. the first principles of natural things.
   b. ethical questions.
   c. theology.
   d. historical problems.

4. Hippocrates thought that earlier physicians sometimes ascribed a supernatural character to illness because they
   a. wanted to hide their ignorance.
   b. believed in it.
   c. thought they were gods.
   d. were taught by Mesopotamians.

5. Thucydides' approach to history may be described as
   a. gullible.
   b. ignorant.
   c. critical.
   d. mythological.

6. Critias seems to have been
   a. a theologian.
   b. a systematic philosopher.
   c. an atheist.
   d. a poet.

7. Sophocles portrays Cleon as a
   a. tyrant.
   b. just king in a difficult situation.
   c. weak and indecisive ruler.
   d. peaceful and accommodating king.

8. According to Thucydides, Pericles praised Athens for its
   a. iron discipline.
   b. austerity measures.
   c. military secrecy.

Copyright © 1995 Houghton Mifflin Company. All rights reserved.

d. open society.

9. Xenophon seemed to regard his young wife with
   a. contempt.
   b. indifference.
   c. affection.
   d. hostility.

10. In *Lysistrata*, Aristophanes is satirizing
    a. marriage.
    b. Athenian politics.
    c. religion.
    d. philosophy.

11. According to Thucydides, the position of the Spartan king on going to war with Athens was that
    a. negotiations should be attempted.
    b. negotiations were useless.
    c. a surprise attack should be mounted.
    d. the Persians should be induced to join Sparta.

12. In the *Melian Dialogue* the Athenian envoys appear
    a. reasonable.
    b. sympathetic.
    c. weak.
    d. arrogant.

13. In his courtroom speech, Socrates was trying to
    a. avoid death.
    b. bribe his judges.
    c. justify his life and work.
    d. stall for time so he could escape.

 Copyright © 1995 Houghton Mifflin Company. All rights reserved.

14. Plato thought that leaders in the state should possess
    a. great virtue and wisdom.
    b. wealth.
    c. political experience and expertise.
    d. noble birth.

15. Aristotle was concerned with
    a. seeing divine intervention everywhere.
    b. repeating what older writers had said.
    c. observation and analysis.
    d. mythical explanations.

16. Aristotle believed that government should be controlled by the
    a. slaves.
    b. nobles.
    c. lower classes.
    d. middle class.

17. According to Plutarch, Alexander the Great was
    a. an enlightened and noble ruler.
    b. a merciless tyrant.
    c. a barbarian.
    d. a failure.

18. Epicureans believed in
    a. public service.
    b. altruism.
    c. self-denial.
    d. pursuit of pleasure.

19. Epicurus thought that the highest pleasures were
    a. food and drink.
    b. possessions.
    c. friendship and wisdom.
    d. popularity.

Copyright © 1995 Houghton Mifflin Company. All rights reserved.

20. The Jews who resisted forced Hellenization did so because
    a. they did not like the taste of pork.
    b. they could not learn Greek.
    c. many Greek practices were contrary to God's laws.
    d. the Jews had plans to impose Judaism on the Greek world.

21. The attitude of Philo of Alexandria to Greek philosophy was one of
    a. rejection.
    b. uncritical acceptance.
    c. critical appreciation, and acceptance of many philosophical principles.
    d. Jewish fundamentalism.

Multiple Choice Answers

1.	b	8.	d	15.	c
2.	b	9.	c	16.	d
3.	a	10.	b	17.	a
4.	a	11.	a	18.	d
5.	c	12.	d	19.	c
6.	c	13.	c	20.	c
7.	a	14.	a	21.	c

Copyright © 1995 Houghton Mifflin Company. All rights reserved.

CHAPTER 4

THE ROMAN REPUBIC

Overview of the Chapter

While Greece was at the pinnacle of its greatness, the young Roman Republic was developing its characteristic governmental structure and consolidating its power in the western Mediterranean. The readings in this chapter follow the progress the vicissitudes of the Republic up to its transformation into the Roman Empire.

Section 1. Rome's March to World Empire

The organizational and military energies of the Republic led it on the path to unprecedented control over the whole Mediterranean world and beyond. The city-state soon became a multinational empire.

In *From City-State to World-State* Polybius describes the unique character of the Roman achievement; he also provides insight into the discipline that made the Roman army into a virtually unbeatable force and maintained it as the backbone of Roman power.

Section 2. The Punic Wars

The epic struggle with Carthage that helped to shape both Rome's self-image and its imperial destiny was chronicled by two ancient historians (neither of whom, however, lived during the Punic Wars.)

Copyright © 1995 Houghton Mifflin Company. All rights reserved.

The reading from Livy depicts the situation of the Romans following their disastrous defeat at Cannae, and their stubborn refusal to capitulate to Carthage.

In the second reading, Appian of Alexandria graphically describes the brutal destruction of Carthage by the Romans.

Section 3. Exploitation of the Provinces

Imperial expansion meant the multiplication of both provincial administrators and the possibilities for abuse of power far from home. The Republic was, however, sufficiently concerned about justice to attempt administrative reforms and to provide legal recourse for the victims of governmental corruption.

One of Cicero's famous speeches, *Oration Against Verres,* is a stirring attack on the corruption of late Republican government. The evils referred to by the great orator will not be unfamiliar to anyone acquainted with governmental bureaucracy, whether past or present.

Section 4. Roman Slavery

As Roman conquests of lands and people continued, large-scale slavery on plantations and in the mines became common. The lot of the slaves involved in these enterprises was much worse than that of household slaves, and generally worse than the relatively mild slavery in ancient Greece and early Rome.

Diodorus Siculus describes the appalling condition of slaves in the mines and the brutality of their rebellion in *Slaves: Torment and Revolt*.

 Copyright © 1995 Houghton Mifflin Company. All rights reserved.

Section 5. Women in Republican Society

The Roman matron held an honorable position in Roman society and gradually acquired more legal rights than women possessed in other ancient cultures. During the late Republic, women gradually came to challenge men's prerogatives in many areas, including sports and education. Some Roman writers wrote sarcastically of the more ridiculous feminine exploits, while others became alarmed at what they saw as a threat to the very structure of their society.

In *Cato Protests Against the Demands of Roman Women,* Livy records Cato's attack on the behavior of women opposing the Oppian Law. (It should be made clear to students that this law was originally enacted as a wartime austerity measure, not an arbitrary restriction of rights.)

Quintus Lucretius Vespillo's touching tribute, *A Funeral Eulogy for a Roman Wife,* shows the deep devotion he and his wife shared, as well as her courage and loyalty.

Section 6. Tiberius Gracchus and the Crisis in Agriculture

The problems of Roman farmers worsened as the empire grew and slave labor on huge estates displaced the small freeholder. The agricultural dilemma would not be resolved by either Republic or Empire, in spite of various attempts at reform. Throughout history, the problems of small farmers have been of concern for governments in all countries, and have occasionally had major political consequences.

In *Tiberius Gracchus* Plutarch discusses an attempt by one of the controversial (and somewhat highhanded) Gracchi brothers to institute agricultural reforms, and the opposition aroused by his proposals.

Copyright © 1995 Houghton Mifflin Company. All rights reserved.

Section 7. The Decline of the Republic

The republican system of Roman government, which had functioned well while the country was small, seemed incapable of coping with the rule of a vast empire. By the first century B.C., moral corruption and governmental chaos were rampant.

In *The Conspiracy of Catiline and the Jugurthine War* the historian Sallust describes the disastrous changes that he thought had caused the collapse of the Republic and the reasons for them.

Section 8. Cicero: Statesman and Philosopher

Among the great contributions of Rome to western civilization was the development of law. As rulers of a vast multinational empire, Roman thinkers were concerned with finding principles of natural law that could be applied to all men.

The selection from Cicero's *The Laws* explores the nature of virtue and justice, and the ultimate sources of law.

Section 9. The Meaning of Caesar's Assassination

The murder of Julius Caesar and the subsequent political upheaval signaled the end of the Roman Republic. Opinions about Caesar's character and political regime varied widely during his lifetime, and both the man and his achievements remain controversial.

In *Justifying the Assassination,* Cicero (who had been pardoned by Caesar) attacks kingship and the man who presumably sought to be king.

In excerpts from *In Defense of Caesar and Monarchy,* Dio Cassius takes the opposite view and attempts to account for the circumstances leading to Caesar's murder.

Copyright © 1995 Houghton Mifflin Company. All rights reserved.

Questions for Discussion or Essay Assignments

1. Compare Polybius' aim in writing history with that of Thucydides in Chapter 3.

2. Is Cato making any valid points in his defense of the Oppian Law? Cite passages to illustrate your answer.

3. Would Quintus Lucretius Vespillo agree or disagree with Cato's views on women? Would Xenophon (Chapter 3) agree with either Vespillo or Cato? In each case explain why.

4. Does Sallust's description of the process of decline of a great power fit any other state you have read about? Describe the similarities in the process of decline.

5. Which of the two views of Caesar's assassination seems more reasonable to you and why?

Multiple Choice Questions

1. Polybius wanted to write about Rome because
   a. otherwise it would remain unknown.
   b. he liked local history.
   c. it was the first European world power.
   d. it was about to disappear.

2. Polybius attributed the success of the Roman army to its
   a. democratic organization.
   b. system of rewards and punishments.
   c. erratic discipline.
   d. opportunities for plunder.

Copyright © 1995 Houghton Mifflin Company. All rights reserved.

3. According to Livy, after the defeat at Cannae the mood of the Romans was one of
   a. calm and optimism.
   b. willingness to make peace.
   c. refusal to acknowledge defeat.
   d. joy at the unanimous loyalty of their allies.

4. Rome's policy toward Carthage after the Carthaginian defeat by Rome resulted in
   a. the complete destruction of the city.
   b. Roman citizenship for Carthaginians.
   c. Carthaginian revenge and occupation of Rome.
   d. Roman acknowledgment of a Carthaginian sphere of influence in the western Mediterranean.

5. According to Cicero, senatorial control of the extortion courts had
   a. lessened corruption.
   b. made matters worse.
   c. provided recourse for victims of injustice.
   d. punished offenders too harshly.

6. The success of the Roman army in putting down the Sicilian slave revolt seems to have been due largely to the fact that
   a. some of the slaves betrayed the rebel cause.
   b. the Romans outnumbered the slaves.
   c. the Romans bribed the slaves to surrender.
   d. the slaves left Sicily.

 Copyright © 1995 Houghton Mifflin Company. All rights reserved.

7. Marcus Porcius Cato thought that in opposing the Oppian Law Roman women
   a. were right.
   b. used appropriate methods.
   c. were wrong in both their opposition and their methods.
   d. should be allowed to speak in the Assembly.

8. Quintus Lucretius Vespillo implies that in his day divorce
   a. never occurred.
   b. was unusual.
   c. was forbidden.
   d. was common.

9. Tiberius Gracchus proposed
   a. more rights for wealthy landowners.
   b. justice for small farmers.
   c. votes for women.
   d. freedom for slaves.

10. Sallust thought that the Roman Republic in his time
    a. was admirable in every way.
    b. was improving morally and politically.
    c. should never conquer more lands.
    d. was threatened by moral corruption and factional strife.

11. Sallust saw the greatest danger to the Roman state in
    a. factional strife.
    b. foreign invasion.
    c. slave revolts.
    d. one-man rule.

Copyright © 1995 Houghton Mifflin Company. All rights reserved.

12. Cicero thought that law is
    a. what is convenient.
    b. right use of the gift of reason given to men by God.
    c. the expression of the common will.
    d. unconnected with justice and virtue.

13. According to Cicero, Caesar was
    a. a power-hungry tyrant.
    b. a fine ruler.
    c. the noblest Roman of them all.
    d. harmless.

14. Dio Cassius blamed Caesar's downfall partly on
    a. a foreign conspiracy.
    b. his insanity.
    c. the flattery of his supporters.
    d. revolt by the people.

15. According to Dio Cassius, democratic regimes.
    a. were the best possible.
    b. suited Rome.
    c. were long lasting.
    d. lacked stability.

Multiple Choice Answers

1. c	6. a	11. a
2. b	7. c	12. b
3. c	8. d	13. a
4. a	9. b	14. c
5. b	10. d	15. d

Copyright © 1995 Houghton Mifflin Company. All rights reserved.

CHAPTER 5

THE ROMAN EMPIRE

Overview of the Chapter

This chapter covers the period from the establishment of Augustus' reign through the final fall of the Empire in the west to the barbarians. The introduction gives a good summary of this important era. Just as, ideally, students should be familiar with the entire *Iliad,* it would be desirable for them to read all of the *Aeneid,* or at least a large part of it.

Section 1. The Imperial Office

The statesmanship and efficiency of Augustus made his reign one of stability after years of anarchy. This section provides two contrasting assessments of Augustus' achievements, one by himself and one by Tacitus.

In *The Achievements of the Divine Augustus,* the ruler reveals something of his political ideals and priorities and provides a catalogue of his accomplishments.

The historian Tacitus in *The Imposition of One-Man Rule* sees behind Augustus' actions and words a surreptitious replacement of republican government by monarchy.

Copyright © 1995 Houghton Mifflin Company. All rights reserved.

Section 2. Imperial Culture

Although Roman culture of the Augustan age largely drew its inspiration from Greek models, it produced some of the great works of Western literature.

The brief passage from the *Aeneid*, Virgil's epic poem, includes a flattering reference to the emperor, who had urged its composition.

The title of Quintilian's *The Education of an Orator* refers to an art—oratory—that was particularly cultivated by the Romans because of their traditional interest in law and public debate. The reading contains interesting views on educational psychology.

Juvenal, one of many Roman poets in the Augustan age, paints in *The Satires* a mocking portrait of lower-class life in a teeming urban environment.

Section 3. Roman Stoicism

Although Stoicism, like Epicureanism, was born in the Hellenistic world, it especially flourished in Rome during the early Empire. Like the Epicureans, some Stoics, such as Seneca, advised withdrawal of the individual from the world in order to pursue personal contentment. Others, like Marcus Aurelius, took a broader view of the life of the virtuous man. The main Stoic emphasis was on an ordered, rational life in the midst of a disordered world.

The excerpt form Seneca's *Epistles* provides a glimpse of the sinister spectacles with which the Romans amused themselves, and discusses the relationship between masters and slaves. The reference to Fortune in the second epistle (number 47) reflects a Stoic concern with "natural law," which sometimes verged on determinism.

 Copyright © 1995 Houghton Mifflin Company. All rights reserved.

Meditations includes a number of passages from the famous work by Marcus Aurelius. This emperor rejects Epicurean pleasure-seeking and stresses devotion to duty as well as natural virtue. his ideas on universal brotherhood resemble certain Christian teachings, though without the spiritual dimension of Christianity.

Section 4. Roman Law

The genius of Rome, which expressed itself in empire-building and government, also developed new legal principles. The last great codification of Roman law was made when the city of Rome had already ceased to be the capital of the Empire, and had fallen to the barbarians.

Ruling from Byzantium, Emperor Justinian issued the *Corpus Iuris Civilis,* which summed up earlier Roman statutes and legal commentaries and preserved them for later centuries.

Section 5. Provincial Administration

The survival of the Roman Empire depended on efficient administration of a great expanse of territory inhabited by vastly different groups of people. Roman governors had to be sensitive to the character and needs of the populace under their control.

Correspondence Between Pliny the Younger and Emperor Trajan is an important source for information about imperial administration. Two interesting letters from this correspondence not included in *Sources* (numbers 97 and 98) might be read if available because they deal with the question of how Christians should be treated and are among our earliest documents on the subject.

Copyright © 1995 Houghton Mifflin Company. All rights reserved.

Section 6. The Roman Peace

The *Pax Romana,* perhaps the longest period of general peace in the history of civilization, is hard for readers living in the war-torn twentieth century to imagine. Although local wars and uprisings occurred, for most of the first two centuries A.D., residents of the Roman Empire experienced no major war.

In *The Roman Oration: The Blessings of the Pax Romana,* Aelius Aristides extols the organization and enlightened government of Rome and the benefits it brought to the imperial territories.

Though a speech by a British opponent of Roman rule, Tacitus in *The Other Side of the Pax Romana* airs his own explanation for resistance to Roman conquest.

In *Resistance to Roman Rule in Judea* Josephus gives arguments against rebellion and lists some of the many lands ruled by the Romans in which resistance either proved futile or was rejected as unreasonable.

Section 7. Third-Century Crisis

Moral corruption, poor leadership, and barbarian invasion accentuated other problems that Romans had long left unresolved; taken together, they brought on the collapse of the Empire in the west.

In *Caracalla's Extortions,* Dio Cassius explains the excesses and irrationally oppressive measures of a degenerate emperor.

Petition to Emperor Philip details the grievances of peasants and sheds light on the chaos and breakdown of public order and justice in the countryside.

In *Extortions of Maximinus* Herodian describes the increasing exploitation of citizens and the people's disaffection with their government.

 Copyright © 1995 Houghton Mifflin Company. All rights reserved.

Section 8. The Demise of Rome

Although the precise dating of the "fall" of Rome is still a topic of dispute among historians, the catastrophic disintegration of Roman provincial government in the west was largely accomplished by the end of the fifth century. The readings in this section deal with circumstances of the collapse and reactions to it.

In *Political and Social Injustice,* Salvian describes the intolerable conditions that led Romans to side with the barbarians and also pushed the barbarians into open revolt.

Saint Jerome's letter, *The Fate of Rome,* describes the suffering caused by the invasions all over the Empire, and expresses the anguish and disbelief felt by observers faced with the destruction of their civilization.

Nearly two hundred years after Jerome's time, Pope Gregory I, the Great, in *The End of Roman Glory,* depicts the continuing havoc wrought by successive waves of invasion and compares it with the vanished glory of Rome.

Questions for Discussion or Essay Assignments

1. Do Augustus and Tacitus agree on at least some facts about the emperor's reign? What is Tacitus' basic criticism of Augustus?

2. Would modern educators agree with Quintilian's ideas? On what points would they disagree?

3. Write a brief description of the type of life that Seneca and Marcus Aurelius would call good.

Copyright © 1995 Houghton Mifflin Company. All rights reserved.

4. Which of the arguments concerning rebellion against Rome do you find more persuasive, those presented by Tacitus or those by Josephus? Give reasons for your choice.

5. Do Saint Jerome and Saint Gregory seem to regret the collapse of Rome? Why would they, since Christians had been cruelly persecuted by Rome and were hostile to its paganism?

Multiple Choice Questions

1. According to Augustus, his official accomplishments were those of
   a. a king.
   b. a consul of the Republic.
   c. a demigod.
   d. an emperor.

2. Tacitus thought that Caesar Augustus had
   a. subverted Republican institutions.
   b. assassinated Julius Caesar.
   c. restored the Republic.
   d. liberated Rome from monarchy.

3. Quintilian considered the most basic and important subject of study to be
   a. philosophy.
   b. oratory.
   c. literature.
   d. gymnastics.

4. Quintilian believed in educating children
   a. with rigid discipline.
   b. with kindness.
   c. by concentrating their learning on one subject.
   d. through a strictly academic curriculum.

 Copyright © 1995 Houghton Mifflin Company. All rights reserved.

5. Juvenal's *The Satires* depict life in the poorer quarters of Rome as
   a. simple and dignified.
   b. dull.
   c. poor but quiet.
   d. dangerous.

6. Seneca thought that spectator entertainment
   a. could corrupt the spectator.
   b. had no effect on the audience.
   c. provided necessary relaxation.
   d. was always good to watch.

7. Marcus Aurelius believed in leading a life of
   a. Epicurean pleasure.
   b. reason, virtue, and service.
   c. self-indulgence.
   d. crime.

8. The provisions of the *Corpus Iuris Civilis* were
   a. invented by Justinian.
   b. inherited from the barbarians.
   c. limited to marriage cases.
   d. collected from earlier legal enactments.

9. In response to Pliny's letters, Trajan
   a. ordered Pliny to stop writing.
   b. refused to answer.
   c. considered Pliny's questions and gave advice.
   d. fired Pliny.

Copyright © 1995 Houghton Mifflin Company. All rights reserved.

10. For Aelius Aristides, the greatest benefit of Roman imperial rule was
    a. an increase of slave labor.
    b. a favorable balance of trade.
    c. the public works program.
    d. freedom and order.

11. According to Tacitus, the British revolted out of a desire for
    a. freedom.
    b. higher wages.
    c. more positions in the army.
    d. a chance to see Rome.

12. From reading the selections from Tacitus and Josephus, one might conclude that the people in the Roman provinces
    a. were all happy and content.
    b. had all revolted.
    c. were indifferent to Roman rule.
    d. included some tribes that rebelled and many that submitted.

13. From Dio Cassius' description, Caracalla seems to have been
    a. ruthless but competent.
    b. harsh but just.
    c. mentally unbalanced.
    d. sensitive to the needs of the people.

14. The readings in sections 7 and 8—*Third-Century Crisis* and *The Demise of Rome*—imply that one of the greatest desires of the people of the late Empire was for
    a. more foreign conquests.
    b. justice.
    c. flood control.
    d. entertainment.

 Copyright © 1995 Houghton Mifflin Company. All rights reserved.

15. The barbarians who overran the Roman Empire generally
    a. destroyed or neglected the old buildings and institutions.
    b. kept the government running smoothly.
    c. left the Empire after looting it.
    d. did no harm.

Multiple Choice Answers

1.	b	6.	a	11.	a
2.	a	7.	b	12.	d
3.	c	8.	d	13.	c
4.	b	9.	c	14.	b
5.	d	10.	d	15.	a

Copyright © 1995 Houghton Mifflin Company. All rights reserved.

CHAPTER 6

EARLY CHRISTIANITY

Overview of the Chapter

The spiritual and intellectual movement that was to subsume, incorporate, and transmit both the Jewish heritage and the Graeco-Roman tradition was Christianity. The emergence of such a synthesis is in many ways surprising. Christianity was based on acceptance of an intensely personal relationship with God and membership in his Church, in expectation of the second coming of Jesus Christ—an event that was popularly supposed to occur in the near future. Under these circumstances, and given the opposition between Christianity and classical culture described in the chapter introduction, a rapprochement between two such different world views seems unlikely. In fact, early Christians made some attempts to forge their own literary and educational materials using nothing but Christian texts—with indifferent success.

As time when on, however, and the world did not end, Christian intellectuals realized their own need for an educated clergy, a philosophical framework, and a clear and precise vocabulary in both Latin and Greek. In the end, they began the fruitful if uneasy cultural cooperation which was to result in the new civilization of Christendom.

The readings in this chapter, which deals with the origin and early centuries of Christianity, represent a necessarily minute

Copyright © 1995 Houghton Mifflin Company. All rights reserved.

sample of a vast number of documents. Included are early texts on politics and morality, and a few illustrating the tension between secular learning and Christianity.

Section 1. The Teachings of Jesus

Since the selections here are necessarily so limited, it would be desirable for students to read at least one Gospel in its entirety in order to understand the context of the texts that are included. Alternatively, a few additional passages might be assigned, such as Chapter 14 of Saint John's Gospel, which points up the characteristically Christian doctrine of personal union with the Triune God. Students are often fascinated by photographs and analysis of what has been called "the fifth Gospel," the Shroud of Turin, which many authorities continue to regard as the burial shroud of Jesus Christ. If so, it provides a remarkable contemporary portrait to supplement texts from which physical description is absent.

The passage from the Gospel of Saint Mark gives one of the passages in which Jesus states the basic principles of his ethical teaching: complete and loving devotion to God first of all, and then selfless love of fellow human beings.

The Gospel according to Saint Matthew contains the famous list of the Beatitudes and Jesus' insistence that sinful behavior is not limited to outward acts or merely following the "letter of the law." The section also includes one of his trenchant attacks on hypocrisy.

Copyright © 1995 Houghton Mifflin Company. All rights reserved.

Section 2. Saint Paul's View of Jesus, His Mission, and His Teaching

The figure of Saint Paul, a vivid and fascinating personality, is known to us primarily through his own numerous letters and from the Acts of the Apostles. Like the Gospels, Saint Paul's letters have influenced literary expression in all European languages and represent an important part of the heritage of Western civilization.

The Letter of Paul to the Ephesians refers to the radical spiritual change which Christians believed began with Baptism—the taking on of a new spiritual life. Saint Paul goes on to explain how the Christian "newness of life" must also result in changed behavior.

The First Letter of Paul to the Corinthians contains one of the most famous passages in all of Western literature, on the fundamental importance of love (understood as supernatural charity) in the Christian life.

Section 3. Christianity and Society

The great variety of early Christian writings illustrates the vigor of Christian thought on all aspects of life. The surviving documents are obviously the productions of minds steeped in the teachings of the Scriptures as well as in oral Christian tradition. Some texts reflect local practices and attitudes rather than authoritative Church teaching.

Sexuality and Family Life by Athenagoras describes the Christian community as living according to a very high standard of sexual morality. The author's somewhat narrow views on marriage, including his strong disapproval of a second marriage after the death of a spouse, did not correspond to official Christian teaching.

 Copyright © 1995 Houghton Mifflin Company. All rights reserved.

Athenagoras' explanation of the Christian views on killing contains the intriguing idea that merely watching a man being put to death entails collusion in his death. It also includes an early statement of the perennial Christian condemnation of abortion as murder.

Section 4. The Persecutions

From the time of Nero until the reign of Constantine, the Christians were subject to sporadic persecution, which became more systematic by the third and early fourth centuries with the empire-wide persecutions under such emperors as Decius and Diocletian. The victims were rarely simply executed but rather were publicly and inventively tortured to death slowly, before large audiences of jaded spectators. In the words of one historian, "A whole society became drunk with sadism and torture."

Persecutions at Lyons and Vienne" gives an account of the torture and death of some of the martyrs, who were of all ages and social classes. Included is part of the touching story of Blandina, the slave girl who, the Christians had feared, would be too weak and timid to persevere in her faith.

Section 5. Christianity Attacked and Defended

The selection from Origen answering the attacks of Celsus is a little choppy, possibly because it is so condensed. Christian apologists insisted that there was solid evidence for the truth of Christianity, arguing both from the historical record (as Origin does in the short paragraphs quoted at the end of the selection), and from miracles that occurred in the Christian Church. Origin is here rejecting, not an appeal to reason and evidence in Christian

Copyright © 1995 Houghton Mifflin Company. All rights reserved.

preaching, but the lengthy and subtle discourse of Celsus's Platonic philosophy as a necessary prelude to faith.

Section 6. Christianity and Greco-Roman Learning

Educated Christians knew the value of disciplines such as logic, rhetoric, and expository writing for preaching and theology. They were painfully aware, however, that classical learning and education were inextricably bound up with unacceptable pagan ideas about religion and morality. The dilemma of making use of secular learning without being contaminated by it has surfaced throughout Christian history.

Tertullian's writings are an important source of information about both Roman and Christian life in the second and third centuries. He inclined to extremism and ended by becoming a heretic. *What Has Jerusalem to Do with Athens?* argues for the rejection of classical learning as unnecessary for the Christian. (Interestingly, when students are asked to write a justification of either this selection or the one following, there are generally at least a few who support Tertullian's viewpoint.)

Clement of Alexandria's *In Defense of Greek Learning* expresses what would eventually become the mainstream Christian attitude toward secular culture. This passage may be considered an early manifesto of Christian humanism.

Section 7. Christian Worship and Organization

Knowledge of the earliest Christian liturgies and community organization is derived from the Acts of the Apostles, Saint Paul's letters, and a number of first- and second-century Christian documents. Surviving from that period are works

 Copyright © 1995 Houghton Mifflin Company. All rights reserved.

by Saint Polycarp, a disciple of Saint John the Evangelist; Saint Irenaeus, who wrote an important treatise on the Eucharist and who had known Polycarp; and the works of several other authors. This section contains excerpts from two such sources.

On the Liturgy of the Church was apparently written by Saint Justin to the Stoic emperor Marcus Aurelius (see section 3 of Chapter 5) during whose reign Justin was martyred. Echoing Saint Paul's emphasis on the newness of the Christian life, quoted in section 2 of this chapter, Saint Justin gives a general description of a Christian liturgical service. He discreetly leaves out precise details of prayers and ceremonies which were not to be witnessed by the unbaptized.

The letters of Saint Ignatius of Antioch, written to many contemporaries such as Polycarp, are another primary source for first-century Christian life and doctrine. The presence of Jesus in the Church is a major theme of Ignatius, as summed up in his famous phrase, "Where Jesus is, there is the Catholic Church"—the first extant use of the word "Catholic" in this connection. In *On the Authority of the Clergy* Ignatius stresses obedience to the bishops and the need to be on guard against heresy.

Section 8. Monastic Life

The original form of monasticism, especially in the eastern Mediterranean, was eremitical—a life lived either in strict solitude or loosely organized to provide for occasional contact with other monks. (Mount Athos in Greece and Carthusian monasteries elsewhere are contemporary examples of this type of monasticism.) In the West, beginning with Saint Benedict of Nursia, a more tightly organized

Copyright © 1995 Houghton Mifflin Company. All rights reserved.

community life became common. In addition to providing for the sanctification of the members and of the Church, such monasteries were often in the forefront of agricultural development, maintained schools when learning had largely disappeared elsewhere, and preserved the classical heritage by copying ancient manuscripts.

The Benedictine Rule provides excerpts from Benedict's regulations which give an idea of his monastic ideals as well as of daily life in a Benedictine monastery.

Section 9. The Christian World-View

The texts in this section introduce the general theme of the relationship of Christians to the world in which they live, and the specific theme of relations between church and state in a Christian society.

The passages by Saint Augustine are from one of the seminal works in Western thought, *The City of God*. Augustine first recalls some of the basic points of Christian doctrine, and within this framework considers the differences between the "city of God" and the "city of Man" which coexist in this world.

The Christian Way of Life by Saint Benedict of Nursia, taken from *The Benedictine Rule*, describes the ideal Christian life in terms which can apply, for the most part, to the life of any Christian.

Church and State by Pope Gelasius I attempts to delineate the separate spheres of two legitimate authorities, that of the church and that of the state. Unlike societies in which either church or state was dominated by the other, the society of Western Christendom would work for a balance between the two powers. This text of Gelasius would be appealed to later on as church-state conflicts arose.

 Copyright © 1995 Houghton Mifflin Company. All rights reserved.

Questions for Discussion or Essay Assignments

1. Compare the selections from Saint Mark's Gospel with sections 3 and 4 of Chapter 2. Are Jesus' words similar to or different from the Old Testament text?

2. What points in the selection from Saint Matthew's Gospel might the Jews have thought to be new teaching?

3. In what ways does Saint Paul stress the new life the Christian was to lead?

4. What principles stated by Athanagoras would be at variance with what you know of Roman morality?

5. Compare the selections by Tertullian and Clement of Alexandria in section 6. Which makes more sense to you and why?

6. Compare Saint Justin's letter to Marcus Aurelius with that emperor's *Meditations* in section 3 of Chapter 5. Why do you think Marcus Aurelius was not favorably inclined toward Christianity?

7. Compare Saint Augustine's description of the "city of the world" with the ideals of the Stoics in section 3 of Chapter 5, and those of the Epicureans in section 14 of Chapter 3. What are some similarities and differences?

8. Does Saint Augustine imply that there will be a permanent conflict between the two "cities"? Could the "city of the world" be converted into a Christian "city of God"?

Copyright © 1995 Houghton Mifflin Company. All rights reserved.

9. What does Gelasius consider to be the source of the emperor's authority?

Multiple Choice Questions

1. Jesus taught that one should show love for God by
   a. looking pious.
   b. going to church.
   c. a commitment of one's whole being to God.
   d. telling the truth.

2. In his moral teaching, Jesus emphasized
   a. exterior acts.
   b. interior disposition.
   c. a new list of laws.
   d. no laws.

3. According to Saint Paul, Christians were to live
   a. a new spiritual life.
   b. like their neighbors.
   c. according to the laws of the Pharisees.
   d. according to Stoic principles.

4. In contrast to the Greeks and Romans, Athenagoras insisted on
   a. free love.
   b. freedom of choice on contraception and abortion.
   c. conformity to the standards of contemporary society.
   d. purity, self-control, and respect for all life.

Copyright © 1995 Houghton Mifflin Company. All rights reserved.

5. The Christians were martyred because of all of the following except
   a. they rebelled against Rome.
   b. fanatical mob hostility was aroused against them.
   c. they would not give up their beliefs.
   d. they led different lives from those of their neighbors.

6. Origen thought that the historical truth of the Gospels was proved in part by
   a. the comfort people found in reading them.
   b. the numerous witnesses to events such as Christ's crucifixion and the willingness of the disciples to risk their lives for His teaching.
   c. the many interpretations that could be given to biblical texts.
   d. the lack of opposition to Christian teaching.

7. For Clement of Alexandria, the Christian attitude to secular learning should be
   a. hostility.
   b. total acceptance.
   c. adoption of what is good and true.
   d. indifference.

8. Tertullian rejected secular thought as
   a. boring.
   b. unnecessary and dangerous.
   c. too difficult for uneducated Christians.
   d. simple-minded.

Copyright © 1995 Houghton Mifflin Company. All rights reserved.

9. Saint Justin Martyr believed that the Eucharist was
   a. the body and blood of Jesus.
   b. a symbol of Jesus.
   c. bread and wine.
   d. the Christian community.

10. According to Saint Justin Martyr, Christians kept holy the day on which Jesus Christ
    a. held the Last Supper.
    b. died on the Cross.
    c. kept the Jewish Sabbath with his disciples.
    d. rose from the dead.

11. Saint Ignatius of Antioch urged Christians to obey
    a. the emperor.
    b. the will of the community.
    c. himself.
    d. the bishops.

12. Saint Benedict envisaged a monastic life that was
    a. purely contemplative.
    b. solitary.
    c. a combination of prayer and manual work.
    d. involved in itinerant preaching.

13. According to Saint Augustine, because of original sin human nature is
    a. capable of nothing good.
    b. totally corrupt.
    c. seriously flawed.
    d. slightly handicapped.

 Copyright © 1995 Houghton Mifflin Company. All rights reserved.

14. For Saint Augustine, life in the "city of the world" is based on
    a. pride and selfishness.
    b. natural virtue.
    c. a supernatural perspective.
    d. altruism.

15. Saint Benedict's summation of the Christian life urges
    a. withdrawal into self.
    b. severity towards others.
    c. extreme penances.
    d. self-discipline and charity.

16. Pope Gelasius I thought that the imperial government
    a. possessed a legitimate sphere of authority.
    b. should be controlled by the Church.
    c. should control the Church.
    d. should be abolished.

Multiple Choice Answers

1.	c	7.	c	13.	c
2.	b	8.	b	14.	a
3.	a	9.	a	15.	d
4.	d	10.	d	16.	a
5.	a	11.	d		
6.	b	12.	c		

Copyright © 1995 Houghton Mifflin Company. All rights reserved.

CHAPTER 7

THE EARLY MIDDLE AGES

Overview of the Chapter

The chaos of the Dark Ages, following the massive entry of the barbarians into the Roman Empire, gradually gave way to a new cultural synthesis of Christian, barbarian, and classical elements which developed primarily in northwestern Europe. The readings in Chapter 7 deal with the conversion of the barbarians, the revival of learning, and feudal institutions.

Section 1. Converting the Germanic Peoples to Christianity

Christianity proved capable of appealing to virtually all the tribes exposed to it, from the Romanized Gauls to the Irish, who had never been subject to Rome. Although many Christian missionaries were civilized Romans, they were generally able to adapt their teaching to local cultures and conditions.

Saint Bede ("the Venerable") outlines, in *History of the English Church and People,* the missionary approach counseled by Pope Gregory I and the apparently mixed motives that guided the English high priest Coifi in his favorable reception of Christianity.

Einhard's *Forcible Conversion Under Charlemagne* describes the final resettlement and dispersion of the warlike Saxons by Charlemagne on terms which included their acceptance of Christianity.

Copyright © 1995 Houghton Mifflin Company. All rights reserved.

Section 2. The Transmission of Learning

The preservation of Christian doctrine, history, and liturgy depended on the maintenance of written records. Also, before intellectual progress could begin after the cultural disaster of the Dark Ages, scholars needed access to the great works of the past.

One of the last Roman scholars was Cassiodorus, who lived under barbarian rule in Italy. His monastery in Vivarium was extremely important for preserving ancient manuscripts. His *The Monk as Scribe* depicts the value Cassiodorus ascribed to that vocation, as well as practical details of contemporary book production.

Section 3. The Carolingian Renaissance

Although the cultural flowering that occurred during the reign of Charlemagne was brief and followed by a long period of strife and decline, standards were set and ideals elaborated which would influence the whole course of Western civilization. An interesting film to show the class, if time permits, is the second half of part 1 of the *Civilization* series by Sir Kenneth Clark, which deals with the importance of Charlemagne.

The brief excerpt from Einhard's biography of Charlemagne shows the great king's thirst for knowledge, as well as his piety and charity.

Charlemagne's own words in *An Injunction to Monasteries to Cultivate Letters* emphasizes his concern for correct grammar and precision in language, and for education in general.

Section 4. Vassalage

The general breakdown of governmental institutions after the fall of Rome led people

Copyright © 1995 Houghton Mifflin Company. All rights reserved.

to enter into personal associations for protection and mutual assistance. The institution of feudalism gradually evolved from these associations, combining elements of both German and Roman traditions. The readings in this section focus on the complex web of personal relations known as vassalage.

Galbert of Bruges, in *Commendation and the Oath of Fealty,* describes briefly the ceremony of doing homage to a lord.

Obligations of Lords and Vassals by Bishop Fulbert of Chartres sketches the principles of right conduct which should characterize the lord-vassal relationship.

Section 5. The Feudal Lord as Warrior

Local groups of fighting men were essential to the survival of society prior to the reemergence of effective government. The medieval Church attempted to tame the warrior class through prohibitions of fighting at certain times of the year and insertion of Christian moral principles into the code of chivalry. By the thirteenth century, some kings had become strong enough to prohibit private warfare.

In Praise of Combat by Bertran de Born presents a number of puzzling features. The glorification of seemingly purposeless warfare, without even conventional references to Christian chivalry, appears to reflect the mentality of a much earlier period than Bertran's twelfth century. The tone of the piece is also ambiguous—is the poem an accurate reflection of the warrior mentality, a satire, Bertran's own opinion of war, or some combination of these views?

 Copyright © 1995 Houghton Mifflin Company. All rights reserved.

Section 6. The Burdens of Serfdom

Like vassalage, serfdom had some of its roots in the late Roman Empire when agricultural workers were bound to the land they worked. During the invasions of the Dark Ages, the serf bartered his freedom of movement and other rights in return for the all-important protection of the local lord. As nation-states and town life developed in the High Middle Ages, serfdom declined in western Europe. Serfs possessed certain rights, participated in village councils and Church organizations, and occasionally rose to high status—Suger of Saint Denis, the great chief minister of Louis VI and Louis VII, was the son of a serf.

The Customs of the Manor of Darnhall details some of the controls and payments to which the serfs were subject, as well as their limited rights.

Manorial Courts provides a sample of local English legal proceedings, which afford a glimpse of medieval country life as well as of the developing system of justice that was one of England's great achievements in the thirteenth century.

Section 7. Germanic Kingship and Law

As it did with knighthood and warfare, the Church sought to Christianize institutions such as monarchy and law. In the process, a new conception of Christian kingship arose, most perfectly exemplified by many saintly medieval rulers such as Louis IX of France and Stephen I of Hungary. The Church's role in anointing kings and, especially, the coronation of the German king by the pope, frequently led to tension between church and state.

The Coronation of Otto I, by Widukind of Corvey, gives an idea of the elaborate ceremony

Copyright © 1995 Houghton Mifflin Company. All rights reserved.

intended to impress upon the ruler, often only a few generations removed from paganism and barbarism, his Christian responsibilities to God and to his people.

Blood Feuds by King Alfred the Great shows the great British king's concern to promote Christian justice and limit, if he could not eliminate, the barbarian custom of vendetta.

Questions for Discussion or Essay Assignments

1. What, according to Einhard, was Charlemagne's solution to the Saxon problem? Would you say the king's action was justified?

2. From the readings in section 3, why do you think historians have referred to a "Carolingian Renaissance" under Charlemagne?

3. Write a paragraph defining feudalism, based on the readings in sections 4, 5, and 6.

4. How do you react to Bertran de Born's poem, *In Praise of Combat*? Are there any indications that the poem is meant as a satire, or do you think de Born is serious in his glorification of fighting?

Multiple Choice Questions

1. Pope Gregory I instructed missionaries to the English to
   a. allow them to keep their temples.
   b. destroy temples and idols.
   c. abolish pagan customs.
   d. force them to be baptized.

 Copyright © 1995 Houghton Mifflin Company. All rights reserved.

2. The reasons which moved the English leader to accept Christianity included all of the following except
   a. hope of the favor of the new God.
   b. a sense of the inadequacy of the old paganism.
   c. threats of force by the missionaries.
   d. the idea that Christianity would provide answers to the basic questions of human existence.

3. According to Einhard, the Saxons were
   a. peaceful and cooperative.
   b. treacherous.
   c. reliable.
   d. not a threat.

4. For measuring time, Cassiodorus provided his copyists with
   a. a sundial and a water clock.
   b. an hourglass.
   c. an hourglass and a sundial.
   d. a sundial only.

5. Einhard says that Charlemagne understood
   a. one language.
   b. one dialect.
   c. three languages.
   d. two languages.

6. Charlemagne was anxious to promote education in the monasteries so that
   a. he would get credit for their learning.
   b. he could listen to learned preaching.
   c. the monks would become civil servants.
   d. the Christian faith would be better understood and transmitted.

Copyright © 1995 Houghton Mifflin Company. All rights reserved.

7. Feudalism was based on
   a. commercial transactions.
   b. reciprocal service and loyalty.
   c. hostility between lord and vassal.
   d. a common philosophy.

8. For Fulbert of Chartres, the obligations of vassalage bound
   a. both lord and vassal.
   b. the serfs.
   c. the vassal only.
   d. the king only.

9. Bertran de Born appears to praise warfare
   a. as long as it is just.
   b. for a good cause.
   c. against the Muslims.
   d. for itself.

10. Serfs were not allowed to
    a. marry.
    b. worship.
    c. dispose of their property as they pleased.
    d. own anything.

11. The coronation ceremony of Otto I may be described as mostly
    a. Christian.
    b. pagan.
    c. Roman.
    d. French.

12. Alfred the Great tried to limit blood feuds by
    a. making detailed regulations about them.
    b. ignoring them
    c. forbidding them.
    d. taking part in them.

 Copyright © 1995 Houghton Mifflin Company. All rights reserved.

Multiple Choice Answers

1. a	5. c	9. d
2. c	6. d	10. c
3. b	7. b	11. a
4. a	8. a	12. a

Copyright © 1995 Houghton Mifflin Company. All rights reserved.

CHAPTER 8

THE HIGH AND LATE MIDDLE AGES

Overview of the Chapter

The civilization of the High Middle Ages, too often denigrated in the past, represents an astonishing achievement. In philosophy, theology, education, politics, science, literature and the arts, the Middle Ages laid the foundations for later developments. By the late thirteenth century, signs of the weakening of the medieval cultural synthesis began to appear, and the breakdown continued during the fourteenth and fifteenth centuries.

Section 1. The Revival of Trade and the Growth of Towns

The town life of the Middle Ages stimulated the development of such disparate institutions as universities, drama companies, and craft guilds. The largest towns were located on trade routes along waterways and their prosperity was due to a variety of business activities.

How to Succeed in Business combines practical advice and ethical precepts, both set within the framework of the Christian world-view.

Communal Rebellion at Laon describes an incident in the sometimes violent process by which the new urban centers gained their independence from the old feudal system.

Copyright © 1995 Houghton Mifflin Company. All rights reserved.

Ordinances of the Guild Merchant of Southampton includes some of the social welfare provisions common to many guild enactments. Besides trade and craft guilds, guild-type organizations also existed for purely charitable and spiritual purposes.

Section 2. Theological Basis for Papal Power

The great church reform movement centered around the monastery of Cluny began in the tenth century with emphasis on reforms in clerical life and in society at large, and broadened in the eleventh century into organized opposition to secular interference into church affairs. In the context of feudal society, in which churchmen often governed large fiefs, their declaration of independence from lay control was revolutionary. A series of reform popes who supported Cluniac ideals brought the problem to a head in the eleventh century.

Pope Gregory VII's *The Second Letter to Bishop Herman of Metz,* which draws copiously on the letter of Pope Gelasius given in section 9 of Chapter 6, together with the anonymous *Dictatus Papae,* represent an uncompromising statement of the independence of the papacy from lay control. The extreme tone of the language, especially in the *Dictatus,* is partially explained by the dangerous aggression of the German emperor—a belligerence which would be maintained by his successors in the following centuries. According to some medievalists, the uncompromising terminology may also reflect a medieval tendency to state abstract principles which were not necessarily meant literally in the modern sense. Unstated limiting principles (such as general consent of the governed, for example) were often implicit in the minds of the authors and generally taken

Copyright © 1995 Houghton Mifflin Company. All rights reserved.

for granted at the time. The technical meaning of some of the Latin political terms is also still debated.

Section 3. The First Crusade

The Seljuk Turks' conquest of the holy places in Palestine, especially Jerusalem, horrified the Christian West. The decision of Pope Urban II to respond to the Byzantine emperor's plea for military assistance by calling for a war of reconquest began the two-century-long period of the Crusades. Some of those who took part in the various expeditions have been immortalized in legends which deeply affected Western literature and imagination—Godfrey de Bouillon, Richard the Lion-Hearted, Saladin, Saint Louis IX, the children of the Lost Crusade.

Robert the Monk's *Appeal of Urban II to the Franks* is one of several versions of the papal sermon intended to arouse support for the war among the French warrior class.

Section 4. Religious Dissent

Medieval Christians considered those who harmed the soul by spreading religious error to be more dangerous than brigands who did only bodily harm. Most of the major heretical movements of the twelfth and thirteenth centuries espoused doctrines that were subversive of social and political institutions; hence the medieval state was as interested as the Church in suppressing heresy.

Bernard Gui's account of *The Waldensian Teachings* describes the main tenets of the sect; the denial of the validity of oaths was also an Albigensian doctrine.

The establishment of the Inquisition had as one of its aims the replacement of irregular anti-heretic trials and lynch mobs with systematic legal investigation. Distinctions

 Copyright © 1995 Houghton Mifflin Company. All rights reserved.

must be made between the medieval Inquisition and at least two later ones, and between the procedures of authorized Church courts and independent state courts. Although harsh by modern standards, the Church tribunals were often more just than the civil courts and introduced legal innovations in favor of the accused; their aim was the conversion, not the extermination, of the heretic.

The enigmatic and sinister figure of Emperor Frederick II, author of *The Constitutions of Melfi,* still intrigues historians. It is doubtful whether he actually professed the Catholic faith and whether his measures against heretics were undertaken for any purpose beyond the maintenance of social and political order in his tyrannical Sicilian state.

Section 5. Medieval Learning: Synthesis of Reason and Christian Faith

For centuries after the fall of Rome, Christian scholars were engaged in the slow recovery and assimilation of the most basic knowledge possessed by earlier ages. "We are," said medieval scholars of their necessarily bookish study, "midgets standing on the shoulders of giants." By the twelfth century, the scholastic groundwork had been laid for further advances in thought, and a new analytical spirit began to appear.

Adelard of Bath's *A Questioning Spirit* shows the curiosity and critical attitude of the author, who considers, in the rest of the work cited, numerous questions such as "why we hear echoes," "how the earth moves," "where lightening comes from," and "why the waters of the sea are salty." This spirit of scientific curiosity was particularly developed in England, which became the center for medieval

Copyright © 1995 Houghton Mifflin Company. All rights reserved.

scientific work as France was for philosophy and theology.

Peter Abelard's *Inquiry into Divergent Views of Church Fathers* extends critical analysis to the comparison of theological texts.

Saint Thomas Aquinas was one of the greatest theologians of all time and perhaps the greatest philosopher since Aristotle. The selections from *Summa Theologica* and *Summa Contra Gentiles* demonstrate Thomas's philosophical method and describe the attitude he thought should characterize the intellectual. In reading the first selection, students should be aware that the chain of causality referred to in the first two paragraphs does not place the First Cause in a temporal context, setting things in motion at the beginning of time, since Thomas did not think that creation of the world in time could be demonstrated by reason alone. Rather, the causality discussed operates at any given moment: Thomas's idea is that right now his pen is moving because of the motion of his hand, which is moved by his will, which is part of his mind, etc. Since no one of these things is causing its own existence or motion at this moment, something else must be.

Section 6. Medieval Universities

The modern university system originated in the Middle Ages, as the outgrowth of guilds of students and teachers. So popular and widespread did medieval university education become, that it has been estimated that a greater percentage of the population received higher education in the Middle Ages than at any other time in history prior to the mid-twentieth century.

John of Salisbury's *On the Liberal Arts* discusses the basic curriculum of the universities, emphasizing that the scope of

 Copyright © 1995 Houghton Mifflin Company. All rights reserved.

some of the disciplines is far broader than their names would imply.

What is a Scholar? sums up the definition of a young scholar and his obligations, while *An Oxford Cleric* by Geoffrey Chaucer depicts a perennial, and chronically unemployed, student.

Student Letters reveals how little has changed over the centuries in parent-child relationships, particularly concerning the issue of financial support.

Section 7. The Jews in the Middle Ages

Outbreaks of anti-Semitism had occurred in the Roman Empire in pre-Christian times, and have remained a depressing feature of European history up to the present. The readings in this section discuss some of the medieval manifestations of hostility toward the Jews, and include a passage from the great Jewish scholar Moses Maimonides.

Albert of Aix-la-Chapelle describes the attack on the German Jews during the first Crusade in *Massacre of the Jews of Mainz*.

A Decree by Pope Innocent III provides a glimpse, by means of the types of harassment forbidden by the pope, of the treatment suffered by the Jews.

The Libel of Ritual Murder is set in twelfth-century England, but variations of the same story were also current at different periods all over the Continent.

Jewish Learning by Maimonides illustrates the views of the famous scholar on Jewish education and the practice of charity.

Copyright © 1995 Houghton Mifflin Company. All rights reserved.

Section 8. The Status of Women in Medieval Society

As the section introduction points out, Christianity recognized a metaphysical equality between men and women. Although their roles in society generally differed from those of men, medieval women exercised many functions with a freedom unknown to women in ancient times.

Cercamon's *Troubadour Love Song* contains many of the elements of courtly love poetry, with its idealization of women.

Antifemale Prejudices, from a work by Jakob Sprenger and Heinrich Kramer, is an emotional diatribe that seems to be the antithesis of the courtly love poem. It comes from late fifteenth-century Germany and may not accurately reflect twelfth- and thirteenth-century attitudes.

Christine de Pisan's *The City of Ladies* is an attempt by a celebrated woman writer to answer male arguments disparaging women. The author appeals cleverly to theology, then examines reasons why women are considered less intelligent than men, and recommends ways of overcoming female handicaps.

On Love and Marriage provides a touching glimpse of medieval ideals of marriage as well as details of the daily life of a merchant family.

Section 9. Medieval Contributions to the Tradition of Liberty

Political theory fascinated medieval thinkers, who explored political issues from all points of view. One question that interested many scholars, including Saint Thomas Aquinas, was that of tyrannicide.

In *Policraticus,* John of Salisbury examines and defends the idea that tyrants could, if necessary, be assassinated.

 Copyright © 1995 Houghton Mifflin Company. All rights reserved.

Magna Carta gives some of the provisions forced upon King John by the barons in 1215. Although the document mostly benefitted the barons themselves, it later became a precedent for other attempts to limit the power of the king.

Writs of Summons to Parliament by King Edward I shows the willingness of the king to consult with representatives of the people before taking action in a grave situation.

Section 10. Late Medieval Political Theory

Church-state tensions throughout the Middle Ages frequently stimulated political thought and the evolution of ideas on power. The conflict between King Philip IV of France and Pope Boniface VIII was one such conflict which produced political tracts on both sides.

On Kingly and Papal Power, by John of Paris, argues for a separation of lay and ecclesiastical spheres of authority. The implication of his discussion could be made to support some state control over the Church.

Marsilius of Padua's *The Defender of the Peace* offers an interpretation of scriptural texts to support his radical position that the Church should have no temporal power, and should, apparently, be subject to secular rulers.

Section 11. Fourteenth-Century Pestilence

The dislocation caused by the Black Death was catastrophic. Economic, political, religious, and psychological consequences remained long after the plague had subsided.

Jean de Venette describes the horrifying course of the disease and some of the consequences he perceived in its aftermath in *The Black Death*.

Copyright © 1995 Houghton Mifflin Company. All rights reserved.

Section 12. Lower-Class Rebellions

The same century that witnessed the devastation of the Black Death and the beginning of the Hundred Years' War experienced incidents of class warfare in various parts of Europe. The period following the plague was especially unstable economically, and lower-class discontent flared into rebellion.

The Peasant Revolt of 1381, by Sir John Froissart, describes the dangerous situation in England when a mob drawn largely from the countryside went on a rampage and terrorized London. The rebels were led by men who inspired them by appealing to a mixture of real grievances, envy of the rich, and a utopian vision of an egalitarian society.

Section 13. The Medieval World-View

The section introduction summarizes some of the elements of the medieval world-view. It should be kept in mind that "the" medieval outlook included concepts developed throughout this chapter, as well as attitudes and ideals expressed in architecture, painting, sculpture, and music.

On the Misery of the Human Condition was apparently composed as a sort of academic exercise by the future Pope Innocent III when he was a young man. He said he intended it as an antidote to human pride, and it certainly reports little to be proud of in human life.

St. Bede's account of *Drythelm's Vision* dates from the early Middle Ages, unlike most other texts in this chapter. Purgatory is a place or state of purification for souls saved from hell but as yet unfit for heaven. Although the concept itself dates from the very early Christian period, according to inscriptions found in Roman catacombs urging prayers for the dead, detailed accounts of visions and

 Copyright © 1995 Houghton Mifflin Company. All rights reserved.

imaginative descriptions of the afterlife appear in literature only in the later Christian centuries. In this selection, the ancient belief in the efficacy of prayers for the dead is expressed.

Dante Alighieri's *The Divine Comedy* is great literature—one of the classic works of all time as well as a compendium of medieval themes. The passages given include portions of the descriptions of Hell and Heaven.

Questions for Discussion or Essay Assignments

1. Write a description of medieval city life as seen through the eyes of a feudal lord, a businessman, a craftsman, or a serf. How would your station in life color your view of urban advantages and disadvantages?

2. What points listed in the *Dictatus Papae* do you think would be most likely to cause friction between Church and state? Give reasons for your choices.

3. Compare the opinions of the Waldensians as reported by Bernard Gui with the writings of Saint Justin Martyr and Saint Ignatius of Antioch in section 7 of Chapter 6. How do they differ?

4. What would Tertullian and Clement of Alexandria (section 6 of Chapter 6) have thought of the readings in section 5 of this chapter?

5. Compare the outlook and approach to nature of Adelard of Bath with that of the authors of the texts in Chapter 1.

Copyright © 1995 Houghton Mifflin Company. All rights reserved.

6. Would Saint Thomas Aquinas have agreed with Abelard's approach to the study of texts? Would he disagree with anything expressed in the passages you have read by Abelard?

7. How would John of Salisbury define grammar, in the broad sense in which he appears to consider it? Why would men of his century attach such importance to this discipline?

8. Are any of the symptoms of hostility toward the Jews as seen in section 7 in evidence today, or is anti-Semitism a thing of the past?

9. We know what Christine de Pisan thought of Cato. What would Cato (section 5 of Chapter 4) have thought of her?

10. Compare the picture of medieval marriage given by the Merchant of Paris with those given by Xenophon in section 8 of Chapter 3 and Quintus Lucretius Vespillo in section 5 of Chapter 4. What are some similarities and differences? How are Christian values reflected in the excerpt from the Merchant of Paris?

11. On what points would Pope Gelasius I (section 9 of Chapter 6) have agreed with John of Paris? Where would they differ?

12. How would you explain the emergence and behavior of the Flagellants?

13. What common elements do you find in the selections from St. Bede and Dante? How do you account for similarities in texts produced five centuries apart?

 Copyright © 1995 Houghton Mifflin Company. All rights reserved.

14. Would Dante agree with Cicero or with Dio Cassius (section 9, Chapter 4) on the assassination of Julius Caesar?

Multiple Choice Questions

1. The author of *How to Succeed in Business* believed in
   a. cheating without getting caught.
   b. devoting all one's time to business.
   c. a pious, honest, active life.
   d. learning from experience, not from books.

2. Abbot Guibert thought King Louis VI was
   a. totally corrupt.
   b. generally good, but influenced by bad people.
   c. correct in his actions concerning Laon.
   d. not involved in any way in the affairs of Laon.

3. A guildsman received all of the following benefits from guild membership except
   a. legal assistance.
   b. help in sickness or unemployment.
   c. protection against competition.
   d. freedom to run his business with no regulation.

4. According to Pope Gregory VII, the issue which caused him to write to Bishop Herman was his
   a. desire for world power.
   b. right to take action against the German king's attacks on the Church.
   c. renunciation of papal authority.
   d. desire to make concessions to the German king.

Copyright © 1995 Houghton Mifflin Company. All rights reserved.

5. The first Crusade was intended to
   a. convert the Muslims.
   b. destroy the Byzantine Empire.
   c. conquer Persia.
   d. recover the Christian holy places.

6. The Waldensians believed in
   a. authority of the Church.
   b. validity of solemn oaths.
   c. preaching by example rather than words.
   d. priesthood of men and women of their sect alone.

7. Adelard of Bath believed in approaching the study of nature
   a. mythologically.
   b. poetically.
   c. by means of authority.
   d. rationally.

8. Peter Abelard urged an approach to ancient texts that was
   a. critical and analytical.
   b. unquestioning.
   c. allegorical.
   d. careless.

9. Saint Thomas Aquinas, in discussing the existence of God, appeals to principles of
   a. authority.
   b. philosophy.
   c. tradition.
   d. mythology.

10. Aquinas held that the human will is
   a. genetically determined.
   b. determined by God.
   c. free.
   d. predestined.

 Copyright © 1995 Houghton Mifflin Company. All rights reserved.

11. Chaucer's Oxford Cleric found in education
    a. a government job.
    b. poverty and a love of study.
    c. wealth.
    d. a lucrative teaching career.

12. The Merchant of Paris considered the roles of husbands and wives in marriage as
    a. unequal, in that husbands had no obligations.
    b. the same in every respect.
    c. unimportant, because married life was unimportant.
    d. essentially equal, though differing in details.

13. Medieval theorists considered political authority to be regulated and limited primarily by
    a. custom.
    b. power.
    c. nothing.
    d. law.

14. In searching for the causes of the Black Death, many people decided the infection was spread by
    a. fleas.
    b. a virus.
    c. children.
    d. well water poisoned by Jews.

15. John Ball called for
    a. limited social reforms.
    b. egalitarian revolution.
    c. more capitalism.
    d. a stronger monarchy.

Copyright © 1995 Houghton Mifflin Company. All rights reserved.

Multiple Choice Answers

1. c
2. b
3. d
4. b
5. d
6. d
7. d
8. a
9. b
10. c
11. b
12. d
13. d
14. d
15. b

 Copyright © 1995 Houghton Mifflin Company. All rights reserved.

CHAPTER 9

THE RENAISSANCE

Overview of the Chapter

European society in the late thirteenth century began to show signs of a growing worldliness and pursuit of material prosperity, and a corresponding apathy toward spiritual matters. Heresy, church-state conflict, and the war, disease and famines of the fourteenth century combined to weaken the medieval cultural synthesis. Beginning with the writings of the Renaissance humanists, a new outlook on both human nature and society began to emerge.

Man in medieval society was seen as a person possessed of great dignity by virtue of his relationship to God. He was not, however, generally considered in complete isolation from the community at large. He lived his life in a rich complex of human relations (with family, guild, commune, Church, etc.) which helped to define him as an individual. Renaissance writings, however, gradually began to reflect a new concept of the independent, autonomous individual—an idea that was to develop into a major theme of the modern mentality.

Section 1. The Humanists' Fascination with Antiquity

The selections in this section illustrate the Renaissance fascination with Greek and Roman literature, originally due to a linguistic preference for classical Latin over medieval

Copyright © 1995 Houghton Mifflin Company. All rights reserved.

Latin, but later extending to the ideals, tastes, and morals of the classical pagan world—or as the humanists imagined that world to have been. The love for and study of ancient literature was by no means new. Even before the great revivals of the twelfth and thirteenth centuries, Latin (and some Greek) literature had been known in the West through monastic manuscripts, although by Petrarch's time literary and oratorical studies had lost ground to the taste for Aristotelian philosophy and Roman law. What many Renaissance humanists found in classical literature, however, was not what the medieval scholars had found; the humanists culled from the ancient texts ideas which reflected their own emphasis on individualism and a man-centered world.

The first reading is part of Petrarch's rhetorical complaint about the literary ignorance of his contemporaries. The text gives an idea, not only of the authors the "father of humanism" venerated, but also of the passion with which he pleaded the cause of classical learning.

The excerpts from the writings of Leonardo Bruni echo Petrarch's concern for the pursuit of classical studies, and provide an interesting example of a humanist's ideal curriculum. Theology is not even mentioned, philosophy is not stressed, but history is given pride of place—a complete reversal of medieval educational priorities.

Section 2. Human Dignity

The one text included here is significant for several reasons. Pico della Mirandola expresses in flamboyant style the Renaissance optimistic view of human nature. Mingling biblical and classical texts, he gives an account of God's creation which removes man from the hierarchy of being and attributes to him a perfection

 Copyright © 1995 Houghton Mifflin Company. All rights reserved.

beyond that of any other creature including angels. Pico's human being appears as the ultimate individual—a creature of no fixed essence who is invited by God to create himself. By choosing the process of self-creation over the fixed status of any other creature, man attains union with God (though not in the Christian sense) and rises above all things—has he thus come to equal God?

Section 3. Celebration of the Worldly Life

In some ways, much of Renaissance thought represents a direct contradiction of the spiritual orientation of both the Hebrews (see Chapter 2) and Christians (see Chapters 6 though 8). In its focus on man and the world rather than "the infinite horizon" of Judaeo-Christian thought, some of Renaissance writing resembles both the work of classical authors and Saint Augustine's stern description of "the city of the world" in section 9 of Chapter 6.

The first excerpt from *Gargantua and Pantagruel* by Rabelais explicitly rejects Christian asceticism. The second passage oddly recommends Scripture as a subject for study, although it is not clear what Pantagruel was supposed to find in the teachings of the Hebrew ethical writers or in those of Jesus Christ.

Section 4. Break with Medieval Political Theory

Noccolò Machiavelli's *The Prince* is one of the most famous (or infamous) books ever written in Western Europe. It represents a departure not only from Christian principles but from Hebrew, Greek, and Roman political thought as well. The excerpts provided in section 4 give some idea of the novelty of Machiavelli's ideas on politics, but also his cynical view of man. The

Copyright © 1995 Houghton Mifflin Company. All rights reserved.

principles of the "new morality" to be found in *The Prince*, whether explicitly stated or implied, have exercised a perennial fascination on readers ever since the book first appeared—each generation has found them oddly contemporary. Machiavelli stimulates thought about the most basic philosophical and moral questions: What is the end of man? What is the nature of political society? Does the end justify the means? Is the survival of a given political regime an end in itself? Are moral principles nothing but impossible ideals which should interfere as little as possible with "real life"?

Section 5. Renaissance Art

Renaissance artists linked mathematics and science with art to an unprecedented degree. While medieval artists had often reproduced natural objects, particularly plants, in meticulous detail, they were unable to solve the problem of perspective in painting until late in the thirteenth century aided by the pioneering work of Giotto. By the fifteenth century, progress in the arts became clearly connected to scientific analysis and mathematical calculation.

The selection from Leon Battista Alberti's *On Painting* illustrates the application of mathematics to art achieving visual perspective.

The excerpts from the writings of Leonardo da Vinci represent the work of a prodigious mind interested in everything from anatomy to mechanical invention. The passages in this section illustrate Leonardo's methodical way of proceeding in his studies, his affirmation of the reality of sense perception, and his use of mathematics.

 Copyright © 1995 Houghton Mifflin Company. All rights reserved.

Section 6. Renaissance Florence

Like the ancient cultural centers such as Athens, Rome, and Alexandria, Renaissance Florence was a city that appreciated the art and scholarship its citizens produced, and possessed a government willing to support culture. It was natural for Florentine writers to eulogize both their city and its ruling family.

In *The Greatness of Lorenzo de Medici* Francesco Guicciardini, while noting some of the faults of the ruler, describes the brilliant cultural effects of his good taste and generosity.

Florence, 1472 by Benedetto Dei is a paean to the glory and prosperity of the great city, which the author defends against its detractors.

Questions for Discussion or Essay Assignments

1. Compare the outlook of the Stoic and Epicurean philosophers read in Chapters 3 and 5 with the Renaissance texts in this chapter. Then compare the Renaissance passages with the excerpt from Saint Augustine in Chapter 6. What are the main points of agreement and disagreement?

2. Would you call Petrarch and Bruni educational and cultural conservatives or innovators? Cite passages to support your opinion. Compare Bruni's exhortation to language study with Charlemagne's *An Injunction to Monasteries to Cultivate Letters* (section 3 of Chapter 7).

3. Which statements of Pico della Mirandola best express a radically new view of man?

Copyright © 1995 Houghton Mifflin Company. All rights reserved.

4. If Machiavelli were living today, what leaders might he consider to fit his portrait of *The Prince*?

5. Compare the views of Pico della Mirandola and Rabelais with the reading from the *Summa Contra Gentiles* of Thomas Aquinas in section 5 of Chapter 8. What is the main point on which they differ?

6. Compare Rabelais' ideas on the good life with those of any ethical writer previously read (for example, Epicurus, Marcus Aurelius, Saint Augustine, Saint Benedict). Which views do you support and why? What would Rabelais have said about the doctrine of Original Sin?

Multiple Choice Questions

1. For Petrarch and Bruni, the most important subject for a cultured person to study is
   a. Greek and Roman literature.
   b. theology.
   c. Italian painting.
   d. Scripture.

2. Bruni thought that, of all the subjects treated in classical writings, the most useful was
   a. religion.
   b. physics.
   c. philosophy.
   d. history.

 Copyright © 1995 Houghton Mifflin Company. All rights reserved.

3. According to Pico della Mirandola, man is the highest created being because
   a. he can think.
   b. he has no fixed essence and can choose what he will be.
   c. he can become virtuous.
   d. he can contemplate God.

4. Pico thought that human nature was
   a. infinitely perfectible.
   b. flawed by Original Sin.
   c. weak and capable of little progress.
   d. controlled by fate.

5. François Rabelais seemed to think that human nature should be
   a. closely regulated.
   b. ordered by the love of God and obedience to him.
   c. detached from worldly pleasures.
   d. completely unregulated.

6. Machiavelli was most concerned with
   a. classical political models.
   b. abstract theory.
   c. practical politics.
   d. theocratic rule.

7. Machiavelli thought a good political leader should be
   a. a good Catholic.
   b. morally scrupulous.
   c. willing to take any means to an end.
   d. sincere in all his words and actions.

8. For Leonardo da Vinci, an artist's work was enhanced by his knowledge of
   a. astronomy.
   b. philosophy.
   c. mathematics.
   d. earlier paintings.

Copyright © 1995 Houghton Mifflin Company. All rights reserved.

9. According to Guicciardini, Lorenzo de Medici's main motivation was
   a. ambition.
   b. piety.
   c. desire for knowledge.
   d. charity.

10. Florence under the Medici seems to have been characterized by
   a. austerity and restraint.
   b. brilliant prosperity.
   c. militarism.
   d. poverty and talent.

Multiple Choice Answers

1. a	5. d	8. c
2. d	6. c	9. a
3. b	7. c	10. b
4. a		

Copyright © 1995 Houghton Mifflin Company. All rights reserved.

CHAPTER 10

THE REFORMATION

Overview of the Chapter

The Reformation was an extremely complex phenomenon in which politics, nationalism, economics, and class interests became mingled with purely religious concerns. As the chapter introduction points out, the Reformation led to increasing secularization of society; it was, however, also preceded and at least partially caused by secularization.

Already in the late Middle Ages, as one historian of that period has written of people increasingly interested in worldly goods, "They began to keep two sets of books—one for themselves and one for God." A more worldly life led many people to chafe under Catholic economic restrictions: prohibitions against usury, guild regulations, lack of prestige accorded the successful businessman.

If it is true that a genuine thirst for spirituality existed, along with a desire to see the elimination of the worldliness and corruption of many churchman, many other factors also combined to turn the movement for moral reform into the proclamation of new doctrines and new religions.

Copyright © 1995 Houghton Mifflin Company. All rights reserved.

Section 1. Late Medieval Attempts to Reform the Church

The lowering of moral standards and psychological instability caused by the disasters of the fourteenth century (Black Death, Hundred Years' War, Great Schism) affected the institutional Church as well as secular society. Reforms in many areas were sorely needed but slow in coming, and were hampered by lack of leadership from the papacy as well as by the absence of dynamic new religious orders. In northern Europe, some attempts at reform were made, but they were too little and too late to prevent the upheaval of the Reformation.

One of the great spiritual classics of all time is *The Imitation of Christ* by Thomas à Kempis. The excerpt in this section gives an idea of the author's approach to spirituality and his practical advice for drawing nearer to God.

Section 2. A Catholic Critic of the Church

Although Erasmus, humanist and friend of Thomas More, did not leave the Catholic Church or wholeheartedly support the Reformation, his caustic attacks on the Catholic clergy provided ammunition for its enemies.

In Praise of Folly rails against clerical ignorance and superstitious practices used as substitutes for virtue and holiness of life.

Section 3. The Lutheran Reformation

The Reformation of the sixteenth century was a complex phenomenon which included far more than the career of Martin Luther. The selections given here, however, summarize some of the themes which characterize much of the thought of this period, and which would have important

 Copyright © 1995 Houghton Mifflin Company. All rights reserved.

ramifications in politics, ethics, economics, and psychology, as well as in religion.

On Papal Power expresses Luther's rejection of the principle of a permanent, divinely instituted authority in the Church. This was not only a clear break with the Roman Catholic Church, but also, it spawned intense controversy among Protestants over the nature of ecclesiastical authority as new sects proliferated. By implication, the debate could be extended to include the question of authority in the state.

In *Justification of Faith,* Luther states his famous doctrine that faith alone suffices for salvation; "good works," although somehow required by God, could not affect one's prospects of being saved. Note that in this excerpt we are not given Luther's definition of faith, which differs considerably from the traditional Catholic definition. It would be worthwhile to compare the two definitions (a class project, perhaps) before reading the text.

The Interpretation of the Bible opposes two points of Catholic teaching: (1) that the pope (the successor of the Apostle Peter) is the final authority on the meaning of Scripture, and (2) that the priesthood is a sacrament conferred only by a bishop. Luther's views, which he himself did not fully implement and sometimes contradicted in practice, imply a subjective, individualistic approach to the interpretation of Scripture, with each person deciding its meaning for himself, and a democratic church organization in which authority resides in the members.

Section 4. The German Peasants' Revolt

As Erasmus' mocking attacks on the clergy and on religious practices provided ammunition for

Copyright © 1995 Houghton Mifflin Company. All rights reserved.

the Lutherans, so Protestant doctrines would have unintended repercussions in many spheres. Thus, German peasants understood Luther's ideas to sanction revolt against oppression. On the other hand, some recent writers have seen in Luther's largely unqualified support for political rulers a basis for later German authoritarianism.

The Twelve Articles selection is a very interesting mixture of clear statements of peasant complaints, an apparent desire to base social organization on a literal interpretation of certain Scriptural texts, and an assertion of power to elect spiritual, and possibly political, leaders.

Luther's *Against the Peasants* encourages the ruthless suppression of the rebellion. In some passages Luther opposes the peasants' interpretation of Scripture with his own—a hint of the growing Protestant dilemma over subjective determination of the meaning of Scripture.

Section 5. Luther and the Jews

Anti-Jewish sentiment, which Luther both reflected and exploited, had always existed in Europe, even in the pre-Christian Roman Empire. Catholic preachers, such as Saint Vincent Ferrer in the fifteenth century, attempted to convert the Jews, with some small success, but had warned against forcible conversion or persecution on the grounds that a human being's conscience must never be forced (see section 7 of Chapter 8). Jewish communities, synagogues, schools, and civil law courts were not to be molested.

On the Jews and Their Lies is a vindictive diatribe against the Jews that expresses many traditional grievances against them, and calls for the destruction of both synagogues and Jewish dwellings.

 Copyright © 1995 Houghton Mifflin Company. All rights reserved.

Section 6. The Anabaptists and the Case for Religious Liberty

The development of the Anabaptist sect was part of the fragmentation that was to plague the Protestant churches throughout their history. The basic problem was the unresolved issue of ecclesiastical authority in the areas of doctrine and church discipline.

In *A Rejection of the Use of Force,* Menno Simons deplores violence and argues, on the basis of his interpretation of certain New Testament texts, that the secular authority may not intervene in spiritual matters even to defend "the true church." The implications for the theory of separation of church and state are evident.

Section 7. The Calvinist Reformation

While drawing on the ideas of Martin Luther, John Calvin evolved his own doctrines and emphasized different points. He also produced the first great compendium of Protestant theology.

The selections from *The Institutes* include Calvin's famous development of his theory of predestination. Although he cites Saint Augustine, the ideas expressed here appear to be more properly Calvin's own. Augustine had written that "God wills all men to be saved . . . but not in such a way as to take away their free will," a concept at variance with Calvin's main premises.

The role of the doctrine of predestination in producing psychological anxiety and tension has been discussed by some writers, while others such as Max Weber and R.H. Tawney have explored the possible connection between Calvinism and capitalism: worldly success came to be seen as

Copyright © 1995 Houghton Mifflin Company. All rights reserved.

a comforting sign of predestination in the desirable direction.

Ecclesiastical Ordinances gives examples of the surveillance and regulation of life in Calvinist Geneva. Calvin thought regulation and state coercion necessary because he considered human nature to be completely depraved. As he put it, "Man is an ape, a wild and savage beast."

Obedience to Secular Rulers shows the evolution of Calvin's thought from advocacy of obedience to the secular power to justification of revolution. Resistance to rulers "unworthy of being reckoned in the number of mankind" could take many forms, such as the Calvinist attempt to kidnap the king of France in 1560.

Section 8. Catholic Spiritual Renewal

Effective Catholic response to the Protestant Reformation was late in coming. It finally came with the implementation of the decrees of the Council of Trent by a large number of talented and energetic reformers, and with the foundation of a number of new religious orders. The first of these new orders was the Society of Jesus, known as the Jesuits.

The Spiritual Exercises of Saint Ignatius Loyola, founder of the Jesuits, is a series of meditations on the duties of a Christian and on the life of Christ which are intended to lead a person to closer union with God. The "Rules for Thinking with the Church" attempt to respond to the opposite Protestant teaching on the points mentioned. Points fourteen and fifteen recommend discretion in discussion of the issues of grace and predestination. The Catholic position was that God wills everyone to be saved, that he gives the necessary grace with which each person must cooperate, and that there is no predestination to hell.

Copyright © 1995 Houghton Mifflin Company. All rights reserved.

Section 9. The Catholic Response to Protestant Reforms

The Council of Trent was to be the spearhead of the ensuing period of Catholic reform. The Council clarified doctrine, corrected abuses, and called for implementation of its enactments. The acts of the Council would have remained something of a dead letter had not the call been taken up over the next one and a half centuries by hundreds of dedicated reformers, from noblewomen and popes to peasants, who extended the reform principles to such areas as missionary work, women's education, welfare programs for poor peasants, and pioneering spiritual and social work among black slaves and American Indians.

The reading entitled *Canons and Decrees of the Council of Trent* includes a number of statements by the Council on points particularly challenged by the Protestants. These include the doctrine of justification, the sacraments, interpretation of the Scripture, the intercession of the saints, and practices such as honoring holy images and relics.

Questions for Discussion or Essay Assignments

1. How might Luther answer the objection that his arguments represented only his private interpretation of Scripture and therefore need not be accepted by others? How would Catholics answer him?

2. Compare Luther's political principles with the ideas of any of the political thinkers encountered in Chapters 8 and 9.

Copyright © 1995 Houghton Mifflin Company. All rights reserved.

3. From the selections given, write a short essay describing the personality of either Luther or Calvin.

4. How would Rabelais (see Chapter 9) have regarded Calvin's ecclesiastical ordinances?

5. How would Saint Francis of Assisi have viewed Saint Ignatius's "Rules for Thinking with the Church?" Would Saint Justin Martyr and Saint Ignatius of Antioch (see Chapter 6) have disagreed with the rules?

Multiple Choice Questions

1. Thomas à Kempis believed that a person pleased God best by
   a. getting a good education.
   b. succeeding in a career.
   c. trying to be like Jesus.
   d. memorizing the Bible.

2. Thomas warned against
   a. not understanding everything about the sacraments.
   b. idle curiosity.
   c. self-abnegation.
   d. thinking about death.

3. Erasmus recommended expiating sin by
   a. buying indulgences.
   b. touching relics.
   c. repenting and doing penance.
   d. reciting magical formulas.

 Copyright © 1995 Houghton Mifflin Company. All rights reserved.

4. Luther held that justification required
   a. fasts and penances.
   b. good works.
   c. a good reputation.
   d. faith alone.

5. The German peasants intended to
   a. reorganize life in the countryside.
   b. massacre the landowners.
   c. leave the land.
   d. submit to the lords' authority.

6. Luther opposed
   a. the peasants' actions and interpretations of Scripture.
   b. violence against the peasants.
   c. punishing the peasants without trial.
   d. the oppression of the peasants by the lords.

7. Concerning the Jews, Luther advised
   a. tolerating them.
   b. trying to convert them peacefully.
   c. destroying their buildings and robbing them.
   d. expelling them from Germany.

8. Menno Simons believed that the secular government should
   a. use force against heretics.
   b. defend the true faith with force only if necessary.
   c. not interfere in religious affairs.
   d. prohibit all organized religion.

9. According to John Calvin,
   a. God created some souls for Hell.
   b. all souls go to Heaven.
   c. it is within a person's power to choose salvation or damnation.
   d. God wills all to be saved.

Copyright © 1995 Houghton Mifflin Company. All rights reserved.

10. Calvin believed that
    a. Christian life should not be tightly regulated.
    b. people should be closely watched and disciplined.
    c. Catholics shoule be tolerated.
    d. punishment should be limited to scolding.

11. For Calvin, rulers
    a. lost their authority if they acted against God.
    b. held their authority from the pope.
    c. held their authority from the people.
    d. were to be obeyed even if unjust.

12. Saint Ignatius Loyola advised his readers to
    a. oppose the errors of superiors publicly.
    b. give loyal support to Catholic teaching and practices.
    c. discuss predestination frequently.
    d. renounce scholasticism.

13. Ignatius was concerned about the destruction of the idea of
    a. education.
    b. free will.
    c. the existence of God.
    d. human depravity.

 Copyright © 1995 Houghton Mifflin Company. All rights reserved.

14. The Council of Trent, in discussing justification,
    a. declared that it required faith, hope, and charity.
    b. agreed with Luther that faith alone sufficed.
    c. said that good works alone were enough for justification.
    d. said that neither faith nor good works were required.

15. On the priesthood, the Council taught
    a. that all believers were priests.
    b. all Catholic men were priests.
    c. priests were part of a divinely ordained hierarchy.
    d. priests could marry.

Multiple Choice Answers

1.	c	6.	a	11.	a
2.	b	7.	c	12.	b
3.	c	8.	c	13.	b
4.	d	9.	a	14.	a
5.	a	10.	b	15.	c

Copyright © 1995 Houghton Mifflin Company. All rights reserved.

CHAPTER 11

EARLY MODERN SOCIETY AND POLITICS

Overview of the Chapter

The chapter begins with an excellent introduction summarizing the political and economic developments of the early modern period. Colonialism, capitalism, absolutism and, in England, the triumph of parliamentary government are the main themes of this chapter.

Section 1. The Age of Exploration and Conquest

Medieval people had been fascinated by travel accounts such as the voyage of Saint Brendan and the journey of Marco Polo. They were also increasingly impatient with the difficulties of procuring Asian goods, especially spices, by way of the dangerous and costly overland route through Muslim territory. Success in long-distance seafaring, however, had to await a number of developments such as the improvement of navigational instruments, increased geographical knowledge and better maps, improved ship construction, and men such as Portugal's Prince Henry the Navigator who encouraged and financed long-distance voyages.

The Discovery and Conquest of Mexico by Bernard Diaz del Castillo is a lively eyewitness description of the Aztec capital and its culture. Some students might be interested in reading more of Diaz' account as a resource for reports.

 Copyright © 1995 Houghton Mifflin Company. All rights reserved.

Section 2. Toward the Modern Economy: The Example of Holland

The rise of Holland to prominence in trade, finance, and colonial expansion was significant for the economic development of Europe and of the world. Dutch commercial practices often became models for other countries.

The Chartering of the East India Company describes the manner in which the Company was founded and operated, and the support it received from the government.

John Keymer, in *Dutch Trade and Commerce as a Model,* analyzes the workings of the Dutch system and the causes of its prosperity in a report to the English king.

In *Capitalism in Amsterdam,* William Carr lists the business activities which most contributed to Dutch commercial prosperity, and describes in detail the power and success of the East India Company by the end of the seventeenth century.

Section 3. Mercantilism: State-directed Capitalism

The principles of mercantilism dominated economic thought in the seventeenth and eighteenth centuries, and most European governments officially followed its precepts. The mercantilist insistence of considering colonies as markets, rather than as productive partners for the mother country, was bound to lead to friction when the colonists disagreed.

Restricting Colonial Trade: The Hat Act is an example of mercantilist regulation aimed at eliminating American colonial competition with England. The Act provides large fines for infringement of its provisions.

Jean Baptiste Colbert, economic minister to Louis XIV, achieved great success in

Copyright © 1995 Houghton Mifflin Company. All rights reserved.

stimulating French industry and trade, and greatly increased the size of the merchant marine. In *To the Magistrates and Inhabitants of Marseilles,* Colbert outlines the measures he intends to take to promote commercial development.

Section 4. The Atlantic Slave Trade

The development of the trade in slaves between Africa and the New World added new horrors to an age-old institution. Treatment of black slaves was to become far more inhumane than the treatment of slaves in ancient Greece or early Rome.

Memoirs of a Former Slave, by Olaudah Equiano, contains a harrowing account of the sea voyage endured by African slaves destined for the New World. Some students may want to do more research on Equiano, or read more of his book.

Section 5. Justification of Absolute Monarchy by Divine Right

With the breakdown of medieval corporatist society, in which the many political, social, economic, and religious bodies acted as checks and balances upon each others' power, the monarchs of the seventeenth century began to assert their claims to greater power and control over their states in a new way. The ideology of absolutism, as Carlton Hayes has remarked, "was a political idea as popular in the seventeenth century as democracy is today." Nationalism, the desire for an efficient central government, and the tendency of certain Protestant leaders to exalt secular authority all worked in favor of absolutism. In practice, would-be absolute sovereigns, especially in Catholic countries such as France, were greatly limited by customs, laws, traditional rights

Copyright © 1995 Houghton Mifflin Company. All rights reserved.

and privileges, and the power and moral prestige of the Church. In England, however, such checks had been weakened during the Reformation, and with the king as head of the Church of England, religious opposition was at least partially neutralized.

In the excerpts from *True Law of Free Monarchies,* James I asserts the supremacy of the monarch in matters of law and claims the power of life and death over his subjects. At least in these passages, James does not qualify his assertions by referring to his own submission to God's law and authority, as his medieval predecessors might have done.

A Speech to Parliament contains a characteristic justification of absolutism as sanctioned by God. James refers to kings as "God's lieutenants" as did Joan of Arc in a famous statement: "God is the King of France and the king is His lieutenant." James, however, unlike Joan, does not stop there but goes on to recall (twice) that kings are actually called gods somewhere in Scripture—he does not say where.

Section 6. Constitutional Resistance to Royal Absolutism

The Huguenots of France held, as Calvin came to hold by at least 1561 (see Chapter 10), that a ruler who hindered the preaching of their religion need not be obeyed and could be violently opposed.

Defense of Liberty Against Tyrants, by Philippe du Plessis-Mornay, develops the case for resistance to state authority. An influential political idea found in this work is that, while God is the ultimate source of the king's authority, that authority somehow also comes from the people.

Copyright © 1995 Houghton Mifflin Company. All rights reserved.

Section 7. Radical Attack on Monarchy

The English Civil War caused opponents of the rule of Charles I to consider what sort of government they would put in its place. Contemporary English political views ranged from ultra-royalist to near-democratic.

An Agreement of the People presents part of the Levellers' radical program. Included are claims of certain "natural rights" for the people, and an allusion to the people as the source of political authority, rather than to the people and God jointly as in the preceding selection.

Section 8. A Secular Defense of Absolutism

Thomas Hobbes' *Leviathan* attempts to justify absolutism by appealing to the practical necessity of maintaining order, rather than to the will of God (which, however, he brings in as an argument against religious opponents of the monarch). His way of proceeding in his analysis is a preview of the Enlightenment method of reasoning from abstract "scientific" axioms to conclusions about political questions without considering factors such as tradition, religion, history, or concrete circumstances. In Hobbes' opinion, absolutism is the only means of controlling irrational human beings.

Section 9. The Triumph of Constitutional Monarchy in England: The Glorious Revolution

The Stuart dynasty aroused opposition on many fronts—political, economic, and religious. The opposition centered mainly on Parliament, which had long been engaged in a power struggle with the English kings for political supremacy. During the Stuart era, clashes occurred over the sovereign's need for money and Parliament's unwillingness to provide it; over the expansion

 Copyright © 1995 Houghton Mifflin Company. All rights reserved.

of royal control; and, especially, over religion—the Stuarts' apathy toward the Protestant cause on the Continent, their failure to persecute Catholics at home, and their sporadic insistence on Anglican observance for Puritans and Dissenters annoyed various groups both successively and simultaneously. Some Stuarts also had an unfortunate knack for irritating their subjects by their lack of tact—witness the boring pomposity of James I in the selections given in section 6.

The Glorious Revolution, in which anti-Catholicism and political grievances both played a role, ensured the triumph of Parliament: William and Mary owed it their crowns. *The English Declaration of Rights* which, like the *Magna Carta,* was to influence subsequent political developments in both England and the United States, contains statements relating both to political theory and to individual citizens' rights (though it is worth noting that these rights were intended at the time to apply only to "the subjects which are Protestants").

Questions for Discussion or Essay Assignments

1. Some scholars have argued that the development and expansion of European capitalism and colonial enterprises in the sixteenth and seventeenth centuries inevitably led to exploitation and suffering for the rest of the world. Do you agree with this assessment, or do you see anything positive in the increasing global dominance of Europe? How could European economic expansion have proceeded according to more humane principles?

Copyright © 1995 Houghton Mifflin Company. All rights reserved.

2. In his defense of absolute monarchy, James I appears both to agree with some earlier political theorists and to go beyond them. Compare his ideas with those expressed by one or more of the following: Pope Gelasius I (section 9 of Chapter 6), Pope Gregory VII (section 2 of Chapter 8), the authors of the passages in section 9 of Chapter 8, Machiavelli (section 4 of Chapter 9), Martin Luther or John Calvin (sections 4 and 7 of Chapter 10). Do you find points in James' treatise that were not made by the other writers?

3. Philippe du Plessis-Mornay held that it was "permissible to resist a prince who is a violator of God's law." Who would he say has the right to determine whether or not God's law has been violated?

4. Would Hobbes agree with Machiavelli's view (section 4, Chapter 9) of human nature? Would Machiavelli agree with Hobbes' solution to the problem of the best form of government?

5. Do you agree with Hobbes' views of human nature and society? If not, on what grounds would you argue against them?

Multiple Choice Questions

1. Diaz and Cortez admired all of the following Aztec characteristics except their
   a. organization.
   b. building skills.
   c. cleanliness.
   d. religion.

 Copyright © 1995 Houghton Mifflin Company. All rights reserved.

2. John Keymer thought that Dutch prosperity was due to all of the following except
   a. higher tariffs and customs duties.
   b. their success as middlemen.
   c. the fishing industry.
   d. their aggressive pursuit of trade opportunities.

3. The Hat Act was intended to
   a. stimulate American production of hats.
   b. stop all hat-making in England.
   c. regulate imports of hats from France.
   d. stop American manufacture of hats.

4. According to Olaudah Equiano, one of the worst sufferings the slaves endured was
   a. beatings.
   b. separation from loved ones.
   c. sickness.
   d. overcrowding in the ships.

5. James I stated, concerning the "just grievances" of his subjects, that
   a. no such grievances existed.
   b. he did not want to hear about them.
   c. he wanted to be informed about them.
   d. they were the fault of Parliament.

6. James I was concerned with preserving
   a. his royal prerogatives and freedom of action.
   b. the rights of Parliament.
   c. a figurehead monarchy.
   d. an equal partnership of king and Parliament.

Copyright © 1995 Houghton Mifflin Company. All rights reserved.

7. Philippe du Plessis-Mornay held that political authority came to the ruler from
   a. God alone.
   b. the state of nature.
   c. the pope.
   d. God and the people.

8. The Levellers argued that political authority was limited by
   a. the ruler.
   b. natural rights.
   c. Parliament.
   d. the Anglican Church.

9. The Levellers thought that members of Parliament should be chosen by
   a. the people, for long terms.
   b. the people, for short terms.
   c. the ruler.
   d. a committee of Levellers.

10. In Thomas Hobbes' view, human beings are by nature
   a. unequal.
   b. generally equal.
   c. friendly toward each other.
   d. peaceful.

11. Hobbes saw the "state of nature" as characterized by
   a. tranquility.
   b. prosperity.
   c. warfare.
   d. democratic process.

12. James I and Thomas Hobbes believed in
   a. a multi-party democracy.
   b. socialism.
   c. absolutism.
   d. the state of nature.

 Copyright © 1995 Houghton Mifflin Company. All rights reserved.

13. The English Declaration of Rights emphasized the increased power of
    a. Catholics.
    b. Parliament.
    c. William of Orange.
    d. common men and women.

14. The English Declaration of Rights upheld
    a. limited monarchy.
    b. parliamentary democracy.
    c. dictatorship.
    d. equal rights for all citizens.

Multiple Choice Answers

1. d
2. a
3. d
4. b
5. c
6. a
7. d
8. b
9. b
10. b
11. c
12. c
13. b
14. a

Copyright © 1995 Houghton Mifflin Company. All rights reserved.

CHAPTER 12

THE SCIENTIFIC REVOLUTION

Overview of the Chapter

The crucial importance of the Scientific Revolution to an understanding of modern thought is not limited to the realm of science. In addition to the great advances made in the purely scientific developments of this period, greatly facilitated by earlier advances in mathematics and the making of scientific instruments, the "Revolution" contributed to a changed mentality in several areas. As the chapter introduction makes clear, the methods of the sixteenth- and seventeenth-century scientists were not totally new; ancient Greek thinkers and their medieval successors, especially in England, had used a combination of deductive and inductive methods in studying the natural world. What was new, however, was a shift in the approach to the uses of natural science in at least four areas: (1) the new scientists, unlike ancient and medieval thinkers, tended to focus on the *how* of physical processes rather than the ultimate *why* (final causation)—descriptions of natural laws would come to be taken as ultimate explanations; (2) the emphasis on mathematics would lead to a narrowing of the concepts of reason and rationality so that religion, custom, tradition, and so on, would come to seem "irrational"; (3) the rejection of some of Aristotle's scientific theories led to a discrediting of much of earlier thought in all

 Copyright © 1995 Houghton Mifflin Company. All rights reserved.

fields and to the idea (which was later to grip the Enlightenment philosophes) that everything must be examined afresh in the light of "science"; (4) the status of natural science and scientists rose from the relatively low position they had occupied in the classical hierarchy of studies to the highest place. In the new cult of science, mathematicians and scientists supplanted philosophers and theologians as "those who know."

Section 1. The Copernican Revolution

The two readings in this section deal with the first great scientific controversy of modern times—the question of whether or not the earth revolved around the sun. The critique of heliocentrism involved two issues. First, traditional interpretations of Scripture seemed to contradict the new theory, and the Bible naturally possessed a higher authority than the novel speculations of a Copernicus or a Galileo. Second, the heliocentric theory at this time was a hypothesis that had not yet been indisputably demonstrated.

On the Revolutions of the Heavenly Spheres depicts Nicolaus Copernicus' caution in advancing what he knew to be a bombshell of an astronomical theory. His tone is generally moderate, although by the final paragraphs he has grown increasingly blunt and exasperated with his opponents.

Attack on the Copernican Theory by Cardinal Bellarmine provides a good illustration of the Scriptural reasons why heliocentrism was so controversial. Saint Robert Bellarmine, who was keenly interested in science and astronomy, doubts that the theory will turn out to be valid but expresses his willingness to be convinced by "a true demonstration." (It is interesting to note that the pro-Copernican recipient of Bellarmine's letter, Father

Copyright © 1995 Houghton Mifflin Company. All rights reserved.

Foscarini, was supported in his views by another saintly scholar, Saint Francis de Sales. There were churchmen on both sides of the issue.)

Section 2. Expanding the New Astronomy

This section includes excerpts from one of the most famous of scientific writings, Galileo Galilei's *The Starry Messenger*. The reading shows his methods for investigating phenomena and drawing conclusions from his observations, and lists some of his major discoveries.

The excerpts also underscore the importance of technical inventions, in the form of new scientific instruments like telescopes, for scientific progress.

Section 3. Critique of Authority

The readings deal with two issues that were to become increasingly important in the future: the challenging of the church's authority in interpreting Scripture and the rejection of Aristotle. The polemical style of these treatises affords a glimpse of Galileo's often abrasive personality (humility was not his strong point), which could exasperate his friends and foes alike and perhaps contributed to his later difficulties.

Letter to the Grand Duchess Christina expresses the astronomer's concern with justifying his hypotheses, which he treats as facts to which erroneous interpretations of Scripture must yield.

Dialogue Concerning the Two Chief World Systems—Ptolemaic and Copernican raises the issue of unquestioning reliance on scientific propositions found in Aristotle. Anti-Aristotelianism was to become an intellectual fad that resulted in the rejection of not only outmoded scientific conclusions but

Copyright © 1995 Houghton Mifflin Company. All rights reserved.

also important metaphysical principles found in the works of Aristotle and his followers. In the *Dialogue,* however, Galileo is not criticizing the study of Aristotle's work, which he praises, but attacking uncritical adherence to a text in the face of contrary evidence.

Section 4. Prophet of Modern Science

Although he did not put his own principles into practice through scientific experimentation, Francis Bacon is known for his wide-ranging critique of earlier thought, in which he goes far beyond purely scientific questions, and his encouragement of empiricism in scientific investigation.

In *Attack on Authority and Advocacy of Experimental Science,* Bacon takes up the attack on Aristotle in a manner different from that of Galileo. By stressing the importance of up-to-date information he implies that there is relatively little to be gained from the study of ancient authors. He does not deal with the question of whether ancient philosophers may have discovered true (and timeless) metaphysical principles, which may reflect an assumption that empirical science and not philosophy is the most valuable field of study—a very modern view.

The excerpts from *The New Organon* are of considerable importance for the history of thought. They not only deal with practical scientific method, they touch on the nature of man, the human mind, and epistemology. The "Idols" section implies a certain pessimism concerning the ordinary operations of the human mind in attaining and formulating knowledge.

Copyright © 1995 Houghton Mifflin Company. All rights reserved.

Section 5. The Autonomy of the Mind

In contrast to those thinkers who employed induction in attaining truth, René Descartes stressed deduction from "self-evident" premises. His insistence on the radical autonomy of the human mind, the uncertainty of sense knowledge, and the existence of innate ideas marks the beginning of the subjectivism and idealism of modern philosophy.

The quotations from the *Discourse on Method* allow the reader to follow Descartes on his intellectual odyssey toward the *cognito*. In sharp contrast to philosophers like Aristotle and Thomas Aquinas, who held there is nothing in the mind that is not derived from sense perception, Descartes's doctrine of "innate ideas" (which are in the mind prior to any contact with the outside world) allows him to posit a thinking subject who has no need of external reality for his own self-consciousness. "I think, therefore I am" is a revolutionary concept in philosophy because it posits an almost disembodied being who can somehow think without taking in the raw material of thought from without.

Section 6. The Mechanical Universe

Isaac Newton's mathematical formulations of the physical laws governing the universe marked a milestone in the history of science. They also, contrary to Newton's own intentions, provided ammunition for those thinkers like the eighteenth-century Deists who posited a universe unencumbered by the active presence of a personal god. "Very few people read Newton," Voltaire was to say, "because it is necessary to be learned in order to understand him. But everybody talks about him."

The excerpts from *Principia Mathematica* include Newton's methodical "Rules" of

 Copyright © 1995 Houghton Mifflin Company. All rights reserved.

procedure for natural science, some of his carefully worded conclusions, and the moving passage on "God and the Universe." Like ancient and medieval philosophers, but unlike some of his contemporaries, Newton considered the question of final causality to be part of natural science.

Questions for Discussion or Essay Assignments

1. If Volume I is available, compare the selection from Aristotle's *History of Animals* with Galileo's observations. Do both writers appear to be scientists in the same sense? Would Francis Bacon approve of Aristotle's approach?

2. Newton seems to assume that we come to true knowledge through our sense experience. Compare this passage with Descartes's statements and Bacon's "Idol" number XLI. Do these three authors seem to differ on the question of how the mind knows? Which one makes the most sense to you and why?

3. If Volume I is available, compare Newton's arguments for the existence of God with those of Saint Thomas Aquinas. Would they agree or disagree with each other on this issue?

4. Write a short essay summarizing the major achievements of the Scientific Revolution and the controversies produced by the new ideas.

5. Why is Descartes' "I think, therefore I am" considered such a departure from previous philosophy?

Copyright © 1995 Houghton Mifflin Company. All rights reserved.

6. Aristotle would have said, "I see (hear, smell, touch, taste), therefore I am." Why does this represent a completely different concept of self-knowledge?

Multiple Choice Questions

1. Nicolaus Copernicus and Galileo Galilei thought that
   a. Aristotle was right about the solar system.
   b. the earth moves around the sun.
   c. Jupiter moves around Saturn.
   d. all biblical texts must be interpreted literally.

2. Copernicus expected his thesis to meet with
   a. general popularity.
   b. misunderstanding and opposition.
   c. indifference.
   d. admiration from theologians.

3. Cardinal Bellarmine opposed the teaching of heliocentrism because
   a. it conflicted with his private interpretation of Scripture.
   b. it was an unproven hypothesis.
   c. he disliked Copernicus and Galileo.
   d. he didn't understand it.

4. Galileo was able to learn so much about the heavens because he
   a. was highly educated.
   b. read Aristotle.
   c. used a telescope.
   d. used the deductive method.

Copyright © 1995 Houghton Mifflin Company. All rights reserved.

5. Galileo's approach to astronomy may be characterized as
   a. based on factual observation.
   b. poetical.
   c. theological.
   d. dependent on older writings.

6. Francis Bacon held that
   a. it is easy to come to know things.
   b. we ought to rely on earlier writers.
   c. truth is impossible to attain.
   d. truth is very difficult to attain.

7. Bacon thought that knowledge was best attainable by
   a. reliance on Aristotle.
   b. random experiments.
   c. ordered experimentation.
   d. self-analysis.

8. René Descartes' formal education left him
   a. uninterested in learning.
   b. content with what he had learned.
   c. anxious to go to graduate school.
   d. dissatisfied.

9. The prime object of Descartes' research was
   a. nature.
   b. history.
   c. law.
   d. his own mental processes.

10. Descartes believed that certain knowledge was attainable through
    a. experimentation.
    b. osmosis.
    c. induction.
    d. innate ideas.

Copyright © 1995 Houghton Mifflin Company. All rights reserved.

11. Isaac Newton was
    a. a formulator of universal scientific laws.
    b. an atheist.
    c. a Frenchman.
    d. the first proponent of heliocentrism.

12. Newton was interested in
    a. classification of animals.
    b. laws governing natural processes.
    c. chemical reactions.
    d. how the mind works.

13. Newton thought the study of nature would lead the mind to posit
    a. the existence of God.
    b. no final cause.
    c. the Big Bang.
    d. evolution.

Multiple Choice Answers

1. b	6. d	10. d
2. b	7. c	11. a
3. b	8. d	12. b
4. c	9. d	13. a
5. a		

 Copyright © 1995 Houghton Mifflin Company. All rights reserved.

CHAPTER 13

THE ENLIGHTENMENT

Overview of the Chapter

This chapter covers one of the important periods in the formation of the modern Western world. The various readings recall ideas first met in the two previous chapters, such as the early Renaissance optimism about human nature, the tendency to consider the person as an autonomous individual apart from the community, the rejection of political and religious authority, and the rise of a secular world-view in contrast to the Judeo-Christian vision of a God-centered universe.

The Scientific Revolution was crucial for the development of Enlightenment ideas in many areas. The new natural science became a cult, a substitute for religion, almost a religion itself. Carl Becker summed it up in a famous phrase: "Obviously the disciples of the Newtonian philosophy had not ceased to worship. They had only given another form and a new name to the object of worship: having denatured God, they deified nature." If nature and its laws represent absolute truth, then they are essential for an understanding of human beings; indeed, natural laws (variously understood) must be the model for the reconstruction of human society. Since the things of nature are most properly studied through the scientific method, which means accepting as true only that which can be verified experimentally, Enlightenment thinkers would demand the freedom

Copyright © 1995 Houghton Mifflin Company. All rights reserved.

to apply the scientific method to all things and to reject whatever could not be proved by it—including the claims of revealed religion and traditional political philosophy. This implicit right to individual autonomy—to pass judgment on all things—is perhaps at the source of the famous Enlightenment insistence upon "the rights of man." It should also be noted that by "reason" the philosophes generally had in mind a more narrow rationalism, based on mathematics and scientific method, than the same word connotes in traditional philosophy.

Section 1. The Enlightenment Outlook

Immanuel Kant, like Descartes, is a seminal figure in modern thought. Although an idealist philosopher for whom things in themselves are ultimately unknowable, Kant enthusiastically supported the use of the scientific method in studying what he called the phenomena of the natural world: "We must put questions to nature and compel her to answer."

What Is Enlightenment? is an exhortation to thinking and judging for oneself, even in opposition to the "guardians" of society (the villains of the piece). The means to this "enlightenment" are various types of freedom—here, particularly, the freedom for scholars to publish their investigations.

Section 2. Political Liberty

The influence of the Scientific Revolution can be seen in these writings, especially in the idea that society should be reorganized according to "rational" natural laws and in the appeal to nature as the source of political principles and rights. (The use of the word *God* in many Enlightenment texts refers, not to the Christian God, but to the god of the deists—an impersonal First Cause).

 Copyright © 1995 Houghton Mifflin Company. All rights reserved.

John Locke's *Second Treatise on Government* has been extremely influential for American political thought. Characteristic of the Enlightenment mentality are the many references to a "state of nature," the idea of the autonomous, reasonable individual as the basic unit of society, and the lack of references to previous political philosophers, historical precedents, or actual circumstances. (In the nineteenth century, Enlightenment thought would be criticized for its abstract, mathematical qualities, which were said to remove it from reality.)

The U.S. *Declaration of Independence* offers a very interesting parallel with the selections from Locke; there may also be echoes of Descartes in the reference to "self-evident Truth."

Section 3. Attack on the Old Regime

One of the best known and most influential publicists for Enlightenment ideas, and an admirer of Locke and Newton, was Voltaire. These excerpts from his work deal with the application of many of the principles of the philosophes to contemporary French society. Voltaire's caustic wit and sarcasm added to the effectiveness of his attacks. Curiously, he was no revolutionary and seems to have favored monarchy.

Section 4. Attack on Religion

A logical consequence of the rationalism of the Enlightenment era was a repudiation of the "irrationality" of religion. Religious doctrines were an obstacle to the construction of a completely new social and political order based on "scientific" principles and therefore had to be eliminated.

Copyright © 1995 Houghton Mifflin Company. All rights reserved.

Thomas Paine's *The Age of Reason* represents one of the most open of the eighteenth-century attacks on Christianity. While ignoring the arguments adduced by Christians in favor of the historicity of the Gospels, Paine roams eclectically among Scriptural texts, rejecting some and accepting others according to how they fit in with his deism. He also discusses his version of "the real character of Jesus Christ."

Baron d'Holbach's *Good Sense* presents the atheist position in typical Enlightenment style, reflecting the prevailing optimism about human nature and the taste for polemical presentation of abstract principles.

Section 5. Compendium of Knowledge

The famous *Encyclopedia,* a major project of Denis Diderot that took many years to complete, contained numerous articles that reflected many of the emphases already encountered in this chapter. The antireligious viewpoint, the partisan, polemical style, the optimism regarding human nature and the improvement of society, the concern with political philosophy and liberties, are all typical of the writing of the philosophes.

Section 6. Rousseau: Political Reform

Jean Jacques Rousseau differed from many of his fellow philosophes (indeed he often quarreled violently with them) on a number of issues. He deplored the emphasis on reason to the exclusion of sentiment and questioned the benefits of life in society—he himself tended to be a recluse.

The Social Contract shows the preoccupations with political questions that marked the age. Rousseau shares a number of rationalist presuppositions about human goodness, liberty,

 Copyright © 1995 Houghton Mifflin Company. All rights reserved.

and the "state of nature," but his proposals for a political order have given rise to much controversy. When Rousseau's natural man enters into a contract with the community, he appears to lose many of his former rights and freedoms. Despite the author's reassurances that the bargain is well worth the making, some later readers have winced at such statements as "the general will is always right."

Section 7. Humanitarianism

The philosophes attacked practices and beliefs that seemed incompatible with their concept of humanity. While some of their critiques, such as the educational theories of Rousseau, were based more on abstract theories than on real life, Caesare Beccaria's *On Crime and Punishments* dealt with a practice still common in the eighteenth century: the use of torture.

Section 8. On the Progress of Humanity

Marquis de Condorcet's *Progress of the Human Mind,* written just before the author's imprisonment by the same revolution to which he refers so glowingly in these pages, is a utopian panegyric to the "new man" of the philosophes: the totally free individual, enlightened, civilized, guided only by his own reason. The first section brings in another theme commonly found in Enlightenment thought, that of the unlimited progress of humanity.

Copyright © 1995 Houghton Mifflin Company. All rights reserved.

Questions for Discussion or Essay Assignments

1. Thomas Jefferson relied heavily on Locke's political theories. Why do you think that in the *Declaration of Independence* Jefferson substituted the phrase "pursuit of happiness" where Locke would have put "property"?

2. How would Isaac Newton answer Baron d'Holbach's arguments in favor of atheism?

3. What does Caesare Beccaria seem to think is the purpose of judicial punishment? Do you think he would oppose the death penalty, and on what grounds?

4. The use of torture, generally condemned in the early Christian centuries, was reintroduced into European law courts with the thirteenth-century revival of Roman law. Vestiges of the use of physical force to obtain information survived into the twentieth century in the "third degree" practiced by U.S. police interrogators. Can you think of any circumstances in which such methods might be justified—cases of kidnapping, murder, political assassination, etc.? Why or why not?

5. Compare Condorcet's view of human nature with that of Pico della Mirandola. Is there any significant difference between them?

Copyright © 1995 Houghton Mifflin Company. All rights reserved.

Multiple Choice Questions

1. Immanuel Kant's ideal of "Enlightenment" required
   a. censorship of dangerous ideas.
   b. freedom for intellectuals to voice their opinions.
   c. better illumination in libraries.
   d. respect for authority.

2. John Locke thought that the source of political power and authority was
   a. the individual person.
   b. the state of nature.
   c. the city-state.
   d. God.

3. Locke thought that in his ideal state rebellion would be
   a. common.
   b. justified.
   c. unlikely.
   d. frequently necessary.

4. The *Declaration of Independence* echoes Locke's emphasis on
   a. property.
   b. religion.
   c. autocracy.
   d. natural rights.

5. Like other Enlightenment thinkers, Voltaire insisted on
   a. monarchy.
   b. censorship.
   c. theocracy.
   d. free expression of ideas.

Copyright © 1995 Houghton Mifflin Company. All rights reserved.

6. Thomas Paine believed in
   a. atheism.
   b. reliance on religious authority.
   c. Cesaro-papism.
   d. deism.

7. Unlike Paine, Baron d'Holbach believed in
   a. one god.
   b. deism.
   c. no god.
   d. the Trinity.

8. If Kant, Voltaire, and d'Holbach lived today, they would most probably belong to
   a. the American Civil Liberties Union.
   b. a neo-Nazi organization.
   c. the Moral Majority.
   d. the Conservative Union.

9. According to Jean Jacques Rousseau, when man leaves the "state of nature" for life in society, he
   a. keeps all his natural rights.
   b. has no rights.
   c. surrenders some of his rights to the community.
   d. signs a contract listing the rights he will acquire.

10. According to Caesare Beccaria, the use of torture was beneficial
    a. to society as a whole.
    b. to the innocent, in certain circumstances.
    c. to the guilty, in some cases.
    d. as a means of interrogation rather than punishment.

Copyright © 1995 Houghton Mifflin Company. All rights reserved.

11. Marquis de Condorcet thought that humanity was likely to achieve
    a. very little.
    b. self-destruction.
    c. unlimited progress.
    d. the restoration of a hierarchical society.

12. For Condorcet, human beings should be guided by
    a. reason.
    b. authority.
    c. emotion.
    d. religion.

13. Enlightenment thinkers in general thought of human nature as
    a. all good.
    b. all bad.
    c. flawed.
    d. neither good nor bad.

Multiple Choice Answers

1. b	6. d	10. c
2. a	7. c	11. c
3. c	8. a	12. a
4. d	9. c	13. a
5. d		

Copyright © 1995 Houghton Mifflin Company. All rights reserved.

CHAPTER 1 (VOLUME II)

THE RISE OF MODERNITY

Overview of the Chapter

The readings illustrate the new ideas on the nature of man, religion, and politics that emerged during the period between the Renaissance and the end of the seventeenth century. All these issues are treated more fully in Volume I, which includes a broader selection of readings from which those in this chapter are drawn.

Perhaps the most important theme to be found, at least in embryo, in most of the readings is the gradual emergence of the concept of a human being as an autonomous individual. This idea can be seen, paradoxically, even in the writings of those who disagreed violently on many other issues, such as the Italian humanists and their Protestant critics. The humanists' emphasis on the individual (at least the cultured and talented individual), the subjectivism of Protestant doctrine, and the theories of the political rights of citizens all represented a departure from earlier views. The individual in medieval society was seen as a person possessed of an immortal soul and great dignity as a creation in God's image. The individual was not, however, generally considered in isolation from the community at large, but was viewed as a unique part of a social whole. Living a life rich in human relationships (with family, guild, commune, church, and so on) helped to define the person

 Copyright © 1995 Houghton Mifflin Company. All rights reserved.

as an individual. Between the Renaissance and our own day, these various institutions that made up the communitarian milieu of the medieval person were challenged and weakened as the idea of the modern individual emerged. Summaries of each section follow.

Section 1. The Humanists' Fascination with Antiquity

The readings in this section illustrate the Renaissance fascination with Greek and Roman literature, originally due to a linguistic preference for classical Latin over medieval Latin, but later extending to the ideals, tastes, and morals of the classical pagan world—or as the humanists imagined that world to have been. The love for and study of ancient literature was by no means new. Even before the great revivals of the twelfth and thirteenth centuries, Latin (and some Greek) literature had been known in the West through monastic manuscripts, although by Petrarch's time literary and oratorical studies had lost ground to the taste for Aristotelian philosophy and Roman law. What many Renaissance humanists found in classical literature, however, was not what the medieval scholars had found; the humanists culled from the ancient texts ideas which reflected their own emphasis on individualism and a human-centered world.

The first reading is part of Petrarch's rhetorical complaint about the literary ignorance of his contemporaries. The text gives an idea, not only of the authors that the "father of humanism" venerated, but also of the passion with which he pleaded the cause of classical learning.

The excerpts from the writings of Leonardo Bruni echo Petrarch's concern for the pursuit of classical studies, and provide an

Copyright © 1995 Houghton Mifflin Company. All rights reserved.

interesting example of a humanist's ideal curriculum. Theology is not even mentioned, philosophy is not stressed, but history is given pride of place—a complete reversal of medieval educational priorities.

Section 2. Human Dignity

The one reading included here is significant for several reasons. Pico della Mirandola expresses in flamboyant style the Renaissance optimistic view of human nature. Mingling biblical and classical texts, he gives an account of God's creation that removes man from the hierarchy of being and attributes to him a perfection beyond that of any other creature including angels. Pico's human being appears as the ultimate individual—a creature of no fixed essence who is invited by God to create himself. By choosing the process of self-creation over the fixed status of any other creature, man attains union with God (though not in the Christian sense) and rises above all things. Has he thus come to equal God?

Section 3. Break with Medieval Political Theory

Noccolò Machiavelli's *The Prince* is one of the most famous (and infamous) books ever written in Western Europe. It represents a departure not only from Christian principles but from Hebrew, Greek, and Roman political thought as well. The excerpts provided in Section 3 give some idea of the novelty of Machiavelli's ideas on politics, but also of his cynical view of man. The principles of the "new morality" to be found in *The Prince,* whether explicitly stated or implied, have exercised a perennial fascination on readers ever since the book first appeared—each generation has found them oddly contemporary. Machiavelli stimulates

 Copyright © 1995 Houghton Mifflin Company. All rights reserved.

thought about the most basic philosophical and moral questions: What is the end of man? What is the nature of political society? Does the end justify the means? Is the survival of a given political regime an end in itself? Are moral principles nothing but impossible ideals which should interfere as little as possible with "real life"?

Section 4. The Lutheran Reformation

The Reformation of the sixteenth century was a complex phenomenon that included far more than the career of Martin Luther. (See Volume I for a broad selection of texts representing a variety of both Catholic and Protestant viewpoints.) The selections given here, however, summarize some of the themes that characterize much of the thought of this period, and that will have important ramifications in politics, ethics, economics, and psychology, as well as in religion,

On Papal Power expresses Luther's rejection of the principle of a permanent, divinely instituted authority in the Church. This was not only a clear break with the Roman Catholic Church; it spawned intense controversy among Protestants over the nature of ecclesiastical authority as new sects proliferated. By implication, the debate could be extended to include the question of authority in the state.

In *Justification by Faith,*" Luther states his famous doctrine that faith alone suffices for salvation; "good works," although somehow required by God, could not affect one's prospects of being saved. Note that in this excerpt we are not given Luther's definition of faith, which differs considerably from the traditional Catholic definition. It would be worthwhile to compare the two definitions (a

Copyright © 1995 Houghton Mifflin Company. All rights reserved.

class project, perhaps) before reading the text.

The Interpretation of the Bible opposes two points of Catholic teaching: that the pope (the successor of the Apostle Peter) is the final authority on the meaning of Scripture, and that the priesthood is a sacrament conferred only by a bishop. Luther's views, which he himself did not fully implement and sometimes contradicted in practice, imply a subjective, individualistic approach to the interpretation of Scripture, with each person deciding its meaning, and with a democratic church organization in which authority lies in the members.

Section 5. Justification of Absolute Monarchy by Divine Right

With the breakdown of medieval corporatist society, in which the many political, social, economic, and religious bodies acted as checks and balances upon each others' power, the monarchs of the seventeenth century began to assert their claims to greater power and control over their states in a new way. The ideology of absolutism, as Carlton Hayes has remarked, "was a political idea as popular in the seventeenth century as democracy is today." Nationalism, the desire for an efficient central government, and the tendency of certain Protestant leaders to exalt secular authority all worked in favor of absolutism. In practice, would-be absolute sovereigns, especially in Catholic countries like France, were greatly limited by customs, laws, traditional rights and privileges, and the power and moral prestige of the church. In England, however, such checks had been weakened during the Reformation, and with the king as head of the Church of England religious opposition was at least partially neutralized.

 Copyright © 1995 Houghton Mifflin Company. All rights reserved.

In the excerpts from *True Law of Free Monarchies,* James I asserts the supremacy of the monarch in matters of law and claims the power of life and death over his subjects. At least in these passages, James does not qualify his assertions by referring to his own submission to God's law and authority, as his medieval predecessors might have done.

A Speech to Parliament contains a characteristic justification of absolutism as sanctioned by God. James refers to kings as "God's lieutenants" as did Joan of Arc in a famous statement: "God is the King of France and the king is His lieutenant." James, however, unlike Joan, does not stop there but goes on to recall (twice) that kings are actually called gods somewhere in Scripture—he does not say where.

Section 6. A Secular Defender of Absolutism

Thomas Hobbes's *Leviathan* attempts to justify absolutism by appealing to the practical necessity of maintaining order, rather than to the will of God (which, however, he brings in as an argument against religious opponents of the monarch). His way of proceeding in his analysis is a preview of the Enlightenment method of reasoning from abstract "scientific" axioms to conclusions about political questions without considering such factors as tradition, religion, history, or concrete circumstances. In Hobbes's opinion, absolutism is the only means of controlling irrational human beings.

Section 7. The Triumph of Constitutional Monarchy in England: The Glorious Revolution

The Stuart dynasty aroused opposition on many fronts—political, economic, and religious. The opposition centered mainly on Parliament, which

Copyright © 1995 Houghton Mifflin Company. All rights reserved.

had long been engaged in a power struggle with the English kings for political supremacy. During the Stuart era, clashes occurred over the sovereign's need for money and Parliament's unwillingness to provide it; over the expansion of royal control; and, especially, over religion . The Stuarts' apathy toward the Protestant cause on the Continent, their failure to persecute Catholics at home, and their sporadic insistence on Anglican observance for Puritans and Dissenters annoyed various groups both successively and simultaneously. Some Stuarts also had an unfortunate knack for irritating their subjects by their lack of tact—witness the boring pomposity of James I in the selections in Section 5.

The Glorious Revolution, in which anti-Catholicism and political grievances both played a role, ensured the triumph of Parliament: William and Mary owed it their crowns. The English Declaration of Rights which, like the Magna Carta, was to influence subsequent political developments in both England and the United States, contains statements relating both to political theory and to individual citizens' rights (though it is worth noting that these rights were intended at the time to apply only to "the subjects which are Protestants").

Questions for Discussion or Essay Assignments

1. Would you call Petrarch and Bruni educational and cultural conservatives or innovators? Cite passages to support your opinion. If Volume I is available, compare Bruni's exhortation to language study in Section 1 with Charlemagne's *An Injunction to Monasteries to Cultivate Letters* (in Chapter 7 of Volume I).

 Copyright © 1995 Houghton Mifflin Company. All rights reserved.

2. Which statements of Pico della Mirandola best express a radically new view of man?

3. If Machiavelli were living today, what leaders might he consider to fit his portrait of *The Prince*?

4. How would Luther answer the objection that his arguments represented only his private interpretation of Scripture and therefore need not be accepted by others? How would Catholics answer him?

5. Would Hobbes agree with Machiavelli's view of human nature? Would Machiavelli agree with Hobbes's solution to the problem of the best form of government?

6. The growth of individualism and subjectivism is often considered a major development in Western thought during the period covered by the selections you have read. Do all the selections justify this interpretation, or do some contradict it?

Multiple Choice Questions

1. For Petrarch and Leonardo Bruni, the most important subject for a cultured person to study is
   a. Scripture.
   b. Greek and Roman literature.
   c. Italian painting.
   d. theology.

Copyright © 1995 Houghton Mifflin Company. All rights reserved.

2. According to Pico della Mirandola, man is the highest created being because he
   a. can think.
   b. can contemplate God.
   c. can become virtuous.
   d. has no fixed essence and can choose what he will be.

3. Niccolò Machiavelli was most concerned with
   a. classical political models.
   b. abstract theory.
   c. practical politics.
   d. theocratic rule.

4. Machiavelli thought a good political leader should be
   a. a good Catholic.
   b. willing to take any means to an end.
   c. morally scrupulous.
   d. sincere in all his words and actions.

5. Martin Luther questioned the
   a. divinely ordained authority of the pope.
   b. geocentric theory.
   c. authority of Scripture.
   d. truth of his own ideas.

6. Luther thought that man was justified by
   a. purchasing indulgences.
   b. helping the poor.
   c. having faith.
   d. preaching sermons.

7. Luther considered interpretation of Scripture to be the province of
   a. the Catholic Church.
   b. all Christians.
   c. a church council.
   d. the pope.

 Copyright © 1995 Houghton Mifflin Company. All rights reserved.

8. Luther supported
   a. a celibate clergy.
   b. a sacramental priesthood conferred by bishops.
   c. abolition of clergy.
   d. the priesthood of all the baptized.

9. James I stated, concerning the "just grievances" of his subjects, that
   a. they were the fault of Parliament.
   b. no such grievances existed.
   c. he did not want to hear about them.
   d. he wanted to be informed about them.

10. James I was concerned with preserving
    a. the rights of Parliament.
    b. his royal prerogatives and freedom of action.
    c. a figurehead monarchy.
    d. an equal partnership of king and Parliament.

11. In Thomas Hobbes's view, human beings are by nature
    a. peaceful.
    b. generally equal.
    c. friendly toward each other.
    d. unequal.

12. Hobbes saw the "state of nature" as characterized by
    a. tranquility.
    b. prosperity.
    c. warfare.
    d. democratic process.

13. James I and Thomas Hobbes believed in
    a. a multiparty democracy.
    b. absolutism.
    c. socialism.
    d. the state of nature.

Copyright © 1995 Houghton Mifflin Company. All rights reserved.

14. The English Declaration of Rights emphasized the increased power of
    a. William of Orange.
    b. Catholics.
    c. Parliament.
    d. common men and women.

15. The English Declaration of Rights upheld
    a. limited monarchy.
    b. parliamentary democracy.
    c. dictatorship.
    d. equal rights for all citizens.

Multiple Choice Answers

1.	b	6.	c	11.	d
2.	d	7.	b	12.	c
3.	c	8.	d	13.	b
4.	b	9.	d	14.	c
5.	a	10.	b	15.	a

Copyright © 1995 Houghton Mifflin Company. All rights reserved.

CHAPTER 2

THE SCIENTIFIC REVOLUTION

Overview of the Chapter

The crucial importance of the Scientific Revolution to an understanding of modern thought is not limited to the realm of science. In addition to the great advances made in the purely scientific developments of this period, greatly facilitated by earlier advances in mathematics and the making of scientific instruments, the "Revolution" contributed to a changed mentality in several areas. As the chapter introduction makes clear, the methods of the sixteenth- and seventeenth-century scientists were not totally new; ancient Greek thinkers and their medieval successors, especially in England, had used a combination of deductive and inductive methods in studying the natural world. What was new, however, was a shift in the approach to the uses of natural science in at least four areas: (1) the new scientists, unlike ancient and medieval thinkers, tended to focus on the *how* of physical processes rather than the ultimate *why* (final causation)—descriptions of natural laws would come to be taken as ultimate explanations; (2) the emphasis on mathematics would lead to a narrowing of the concepts of reason and rationality so that religion, custom, tradition, and so on, would come to seem "irrational"; (3) the rejection of some of Aristotle's scientific theories led to a discrediting of much of earlier thought in all

Copyright © 1995 Houghton Mifflin Company. All rights reserved.

fields and to the idea (which was later to grip the Enlightenment philosophes) that everything must be examined afresh in the light of "science"; (4) the status of natural science and scientists rose from the relatively low position they had occupied in the classical hierarchy of studies to the highest place. In the new cult of science, mathematicians and scientists supplanted philosophers and theologians as "those who know."

Section 1. The Copernican Revolution

The two readings in this section deal with the first great scientific controversy of modern times—the question of whether or not the earth revolved around the sun. The critique of heliocentrism involved two issues. First, traditional interpretations of Scripture seemed to contradict the new theory, and the Bible naturally possessed a higher authority than the novel speculations of a Copernicus or a Galileo. Second, the heliocentric theory at this time was a hypothesis that had not yet been indisputably demonstrated.

On the Revolutions of the Heavenly Spheres depicts Nicolaus Copernicus' caution in advancing what he knew to be a bombshell of an astronomical theory. His tone is generally moderate, although by the final paragraphs he has grown increasingly blunt and exasperated with his opponents.

Attack on the Copernican Theory by Cardinal Bellarmine provides a good illustration of the Scriptural reasons why heliocentrism was so controversial. Saint Robert Bellarmine, who was keenly interested in science and astronomy, doubts that the theory will turn out to be valid but expresses his willingness to be convinced by "a true demonstration." (It is interesting to note that the pro-Copernican recipient of Bellarmine's letter, Father

 Copyright © 1995 Houghton Mifflin Company. All rights reserved.

Foscarini, was supported in his views by another saintly scholar, Saint Francis de Sales. There were churchmen on both sides of the issue.)

Section 2. Expanding the New Astronomy

This section includes excerpts from one of the most famous of scientific writings, Galileo Galilei's *The Starry Messenger*. The reading shows his methods for investigating phenomena and drawing conclusions from his observations, and lists some of his major discoveries.

The excerpts also underscore the importance of technical inventions, in the form of new scientific instruments like telescopes, for scientific progress.

Section 3. Critique of Authority

The readings deal with two issues that were to become increasingly important in the future: the challenging of the church's authority in interpreting Scripture and the rejection of Aristotle. The polemical style of these treatises affords a glimpse of Galileo's often abrasive personality (humility was not his strong point), which could exasperate his friends and foes alike and perhaps contributed to his later difficulties.

Letter to the Grand Duchess Christina expresses the astronomer's concern with justifying his hypotheses, which he treats as facts to which erroneous interpretations of Scripture must yield.

Dialogue Concerning the Two Chief World Systems—Ptolemaic and Copernican raises the issue of unquestioning reliance on scientific propositions found in Aristotle. Anti-Aristotelianism was to become an intellectual fad that resulted in the rejection of not only outmoded scientific conclusions but

Copyright © 1995 Houghton Mifflin Company. All rights reserved.

also important metaphysical principles found in the works of Aristotle and his followers. In the *Dialogue,* however, Galileo is not criticizing the study of Aristotle's work, which he praises, but attacking uncritical adherence to a text in the face of contrary evidence.

Section 4. Prophet of Modern Science

Although he did not put his own principles into practice through scientific experimentation, Francis Bacon is known for his wide-ranging critique of earlier thought, in which he goes far beyond purely scientific questions, and his encouragement of empiricism in scientific investigation.

In *Attack on Authority and Advocacy of Experimental Science,* Bacon takes up the attack on Aristotle in a manner different from that of Galileo. By stressing the importance of up-to-date information he implies that there is relatively little to be gained from the study of ancient authors. He does not deal with the question of whether ancient philosophers may have discovered true (and timeless) metaphysical principles, which may reflect an assumption that empirical science and not philosophy is the most valuable field of study—a very modern view.

The excerpts from *The New Organon* are of considerable importance for the history of thought. They not only deal with practical scientific method, they touch on the nature of man, the human mind, and epistemology. The "Idols" section implies a certain pessimism concerning the ordinary operations of the human mind in attaining and formulating knowledge.

 Copyright © 1995 Houghton Mifflin Company. All rights reserved.

Section 5. The Autonomy of the Mind

In contrast to those thinkers who employed induction in attaining truth, René Descartes stressed deduction from "self-evident" premises. His insistence on the radical autonomy of the human mind, the uncertainty of sense knowledge, and the existence of innate ideas marks the beginning of the subjectivism and idealism of modern philosophy.

The quotations from the *Discourse on Method* allow the reader to follow Descartes on his intellectual odyssey toward the *cognito*. In sharp contrast to philosophers like Aristotle and Thomas Aquinas, who held there is nothing in the mind that is not derived from sense perception, Descartes's doctrine of "innate ideas" (which are in the mind prior to any contact with the outside world) allows him to posit a thinking subject who has no need of external reality for his own self-consciousness. "I think, therefore I am" is a revolutionary concept in philosophy because it posits an almost disembodied being who can somehow think without taking in the raw material of thought from without.

Section 6. The Mechanical Universe

Isaac Newton's mathematical formulations of the physical laws governing the universe marked a milestone in the history of science. They also, contrary to Newton's own intentions, provided ammunition for those thinkers like the eighteenth-century Deists who posited a universe unencumbered by the active presence of a personal god. "Very few people read Newton," Voltaire was to say, "because it is necessary to be learned in order to understand him. But everybody talks about him."

The excerpts from *Principia Mathematica* include Newton's methodical "Rules" of

Copyright © 1995 Houghton Mifflin Company. All rights reserved.

procedure for natural science, some of his carefully worded conclusions, and the moving passage on "God and the Universe." Like ancient and medieval philosophers, but unlike some of his contemporaries, Newton considered the question of final causality to be part of natural science.

Questions for Discussion or Essay Assignments

1. If Volume I is available, compare the selection from Aristotle's *History of Animals* with Galileo's observations. Do both writers appear to be scientists in the same sense? Would Francis Bacon approve of Aristotle's approach?

2. Newton seems to assume that we come to true knowledge through our sense experience. Compare this passage with Descartes's statements and Bacon's "Idol" number XLI. Do these three authors seem to differ on the question of how the mind knows? Which one makes the most sense to you and why?

3. If Volume I is available, compare Newton's arguments for the existence of God with those of Saint Thomas Aquinas. Would they agree or disagree with each other on this issue?

4. Write a short essay summarizing the major achievements of the Scientific Revolution and the controversies produced by the new ideas.

5. Why is Descartes' "I think, therefore I am" considered such a departure from previous philosophy?

 Copyright © 1995 Houghton Mifflin Company. All rights reserved.

6. Aristotle would have said, "I see (hear, smell, touch, taste), therefore I am." Why does this represent a completely different concept of self-knowledge?

Multiple Choice Questions

1. Nicolaus Copernicus and Galileo Galilei thought that
   a. Aristotle was right about the solar system.
   b. the earth moves around the sun.
   c. Jupiter moves around Saturn.
   d. all biblical texts must be interpreted literally.

2. Copernicus expected his thesis to meet with
   a. general popularity.
   b. misunderstanding and opposition.
   c. indifference.
   d. admiration from theologians.

3. Cardinal Bellarmine opposed the teaching of heliocentrism because
   a. it conflicted with his private interpretation of Scripture.
   b. it was an unproven hypothesis.
   c. he disliked Copernicus and Galileo.
   d. he didn't understand it.

4. Galileo was able to learn so much about the heavens because he
   a. was highly educated.
   b. read Aristotle.
   c. used a telescope.
   d. used the deductive method.

Copyright © 1995 Houghton Mifflin Company. All rights reserved.

5. Galileo's approach to astronomy may be characterized as
   a. based on factual observation.
   b. poetical.
   c. theological.
   d. dependent on older writings.

6. Francis Bacon held that
   a. it is easy to come to know things.
   b. we ought to rely on earlier writers.
   c. truth is impossible to attain.
   d. truth is very difficult to attain.

7. Bacon thought that knowledge was best attainable by
   a. reliance on Aristotle.
   b. random experiments.
   c. ordered experimentation.
   d. self-analysis.

8. René Descartes' formal education left him
   a. uninterested in learning.
   b. content with what he had learned.
   c. anxious to go to graduate school.
   d. dissatisfied.

9. The prime object of Descartes' research was
   a. nature.
   b. history.
   c. law.
   d. his own mental processes.

10. Descartes believed that certain knowledge was attainable through
    a. experimentation.
    b. osmosis.
    c. induction.
    d. innate ideas.

 Copyright © 1995 Houghton Mifflin Company. All rights reserved.

11. Isaac Newton was
    a. a formulator of universal scientific laws.
    b. an atheist.
    c. a Frenchman.
    d. the first proponent of heliocentrism.

12. Newton was interested in
    a. classification of animals.
    b. laws governing natural processes.
    c. chemical reactions.
    d. how the mind works.

13. Newton thought the study of nature would lead the mind to posit
    a. the existence of God.
    b. no final cause.
    c. the Big Bang.
    d. evolution.

Multiple Choice Answers

1. b
2. b
3. b
4. c
5. a
6. d
7. c
8. d
9. d
10. d
11. a
12. b
13. a

Copyright © 1995 Houghton Mifflin Company. All rights reserved.

CHAPTER 3

THE ENLIGHTENMENT

Overview of the Chapter

This chapter covers one of the important periods in the formation of the modern Western world. The various readings recall ideas first met in the two previous chapters, such as the early Renaissance optimism about human nature, the tendency to consider the person as an autonomous individual apart from the community, the rejection of political and religious authority, and the rise of a secular world-view in contrast to the Judeo-Christian vision of a God-centered universe.

The Scientific Revolution was crucial for the development of Enlightenment ideas in many areas. The new natural science became a cult, a substitute for religion, almost a religion itself. Carl Becker summed it up in a famous phrase: "Obviously the disciples of the Newtonian philosophy had not ceased to worship. They had only given another form and a new name to the object of worship: having denatured God, they deified nature." If nature and its laws represent absolute truth, then they are essential for an understanding of human beings; indeed, natural laws (variously understood) must be the model for the reconstruction of human society. Since the things of nature are most properly studied through the scientific method, which means accepting as true only that which can be verified experimentally, Enlightenment thinkers would demand the freedom

 Copyright © 1995 Houghton Mifflin Company. All rights reserved.

to apply the scientific method to all things and to reject whatever could not be proved by it—including the claims of revealed religion and traditional political philosophy. This implicit right to individual autonomy—to pass judgment on all things—is perhaps at the source of the famous Enlightenment insistence upon "the rights of man." It should also be noted that by "reason" the philosophes generally had in mind a more narrow rationalism, based on mathematics and scientific method, than the same word connotes in traditional philosophy.

Section 1. The Enlightenment Outlook

Immanuel Kant, like Descartes, is a seminal figure in modern thought. Although an idealist philosopher for whom things in themselves are ultimately unknowable, Kant enthusiastically supported the use of the scientific method in studying what he called the phenomena of the natural world: "We must put questions to nature and compel her to answer."

What Is Enlightenment? is an exhortation to thinking and judging for oneself, even in opposition to the "guardians" of society (the villains of the piece). The means to this "enlightenment" are various types of freedom—here, particularly, the freedom for scholars to publish their investigations.

Section 2. Political Liberty

The influence of the Scientific Revolution can be seen in these writings, especially in the idea that society should be reorganized according to "rational" natural laws and in the appeal to nature as the source of political principles and rights. (The use of the word *God* in many Enlightenment texts refers, not to the

Copyright © 1995 Houghton Mifflin Company. All rights reserved.

Christian God, but to the god of the deists—an impersonal First Cause).

John Locke's *Second Treatise on Government* has been extremely influential for American political thought. Characteristic of the Enlightenment mentality are the many references to a "state of nature," the idea of the autonomous, reasonable individual as the basic unit of society, and the lack of references to previous political philosophers, historical precedents, or actual circumstances. (In the nineteenth century, Enlightenment thought would be criticized for its abstract, mathematical qualities, which were said to remove it from reality.)

The U.S. *Declaration of Independence* offers a very interesting parallel with the selections from Locke; there may also be echoes of Descartes in the reference to "self-evident Truth."

Section 3. Attack on the Old Regime

One of the best known and most influential publicists for Enlightenment ideas, and an admirer of Locke and Newton, was Voltaire. These excerpts from his work deal with the application of many of the principles of the philosophes to contemporary French society. Voltaire's caustic wit and sarcasm added to the effectiveness of his attacks. Curiously, he was no revolutionary and seems to have favored monarchy.

Section 4. Attack on Religion

A logical consequence of the rationalism of the Enlightenment era was a repudiation of the "irrationality" of religion. Religious doctrines were an obstacle to the construction of a completely new social and political order

 Copyright © 1995 Houghton Mifflin Company. All rights reserved.

based on "scientific" principles and therefore had to be eliminated.

Thomas Paine's *The Age of Reason* represents one of the most open of the eighteenth-century attacks on Christianity. While ignoring the arguments adduced by Christians in favor of the historicity of the Gospels, Paine roams eclectically among Scriptural texts, rejecting some and accepting others according to how they fit in with his deism. He also discusses his version of "the real character of Jesus Christ."

Baron d'Holbach's *Good Sense* presents the atheist position in typical Enlightenment style, reflecting the prevailing optimism about human nature and the taste for polemical presentation of abstract principles.

Section 5. Compendium of Knowledge

The famous *Encyclopedia,* a major project of Denis Diderot that took many years to complete, contained numerous articles that reflected many of the emphases already encountered in this chapter. The antireligious viewpoint, the partisan, polemical style, the optimism regarding human nature and the improvement of society, the concern with political philosophy and liberties, are all typical of the writing of the philosophes.

Section 6. Rousseau: Political Reform

Jean Jacques Rousseau differed from many of his fellow philosophes (indeed he often quarreled violently with them) on a number of issues. He deplored the emphasis on reason to the exclusion of sentiment and questioned the benefits of life in society—he himself tended to be a recluse.

Copyright © 1995 Houghton Mifflin Company. All rights reserved.

The Social Contract shows the preoccupations with political questions that marked the age. Rousseau shares a number of rationalist presuppositions about human goodness, liberty, and the "state of nature," but his proposals for a political order have given rise to much controversy. When Rousseau's natural man enters into a contract with the community, he appears to lose many of his former rights and freedoms. Despite the author's reassurances that the bargain is well worth the making, some later readers have winced at such statements as "the general will is always right."

Section 7. Humanitarianism

The philosophes attacked practices and beliefs that seemed incompatible with their concept of humanity. While some of their critiques, such as the educational theories of Rousseau, were based more on abstract theories than on real life, Caesare Beccaria's *On Crime and Punishments* dealt with a practice still common in the eighteenth century: the use of torture.

Section 8. On the Progress of Humanity

Marquis de Condorcet's *Progress of the Human Mind,* written just before the author's imprisonment by the same revolution to which he refers so glowingly in these pages, is a utopian panegyric to the "new man" of the philosophes: the totally free individual, enlightened, civilized, guided only by his own reason. The first section brings in another theme commonly found in Enlightenment thought, that of the unlimited progress of humanity.

Copyright © 1995 Houghton Mifflin Company. All rights reserved.

Questions for Discussion or Essay Assignments

1. Thomas Jefferson relied heavily on Locke's political theories. Why do you think that in the *Declaration of Independence* Jefferson substituted the phrase "pursuit of happiness" where Locke would have put "property"?

2. How would Isaac Newton answer Baron d'Holbach's arguments in favor of atheism?

3. What does Caesare Beccaria seem to think is the purpose of judicial punishment? Do you think he would oppose the death penalty, and on what grounds?

4. The use of torture, generally condemned in the early Christian centuries, was reintroduced into European law courts with the thirteenth-century revival of Roman law. Vestiges of the use of physical force to obtain information survived into the twentieth century in the "third degree" practiced by U.S. police interrogators. Can you think of any circumstances in which such methods might be justified—cases of kidnapping, murder, political assassination, etc.? Why or why not?

5. Compare Condorcet's view of human nature with that of Pico della Mirandola. Is there any significant difference between them?

Copyright © 1995 Houghton Mifflin Company. All rights reserved.

Multiple Choice Questions

1. Immanuel Kant's ideal of "Enlightenment" required
   a. censorship of dangerous ideas.
   b. freedom for intellectuals to voice their opinions.
   c. better illumination in libraries.
   d. respect for authority.

2. John Locke thought that the source of political power and authority was
   a. the individual person.
   b. the state of nature.
   c. the city-state.
   d. God.

3. Locke thought that in his ideal state rebellion would be
   a. common.
   b. justified.
   c. unlikely.
   d. frequently necessary.

4. The *Declaration of Independence* echoes Locke's emphasis on
   a. property.
   b. religion.
   c. autocracy.
   d. natural rights.

5. Like other Enlightenment thinkers, Voltaire insisted on
   a. monarchy.
   b. censorship.
   c. theocracy.
   d. free expression of ideas.

 Copyright © 1995 Houghton Mifflin Company. All rights reserved.

6. Thomas Paine believed in
   a. atheism.
   b. reliance on religious authority.
   c. Cesaro-papism.
   d. deism.

7. Unlike Paine, Baron d'Holbach believed in
   a. one god.
   b. deism.
   c. no god.
   d. the Trinity.

8. If Kant, Voltaire, and d'Holbach lived today, they would most probably belong to
   a. the American Civil Liberties Union.
   b. a neo-Nazi organization.
   c. the Moral Majority.
   d. the Conservative Union.

9. According to Jean Jacques Rousseau, when man leaves the "state of nature" for life in society, he
   a. keeps all his natural rights.
   b. has no rights.
   c. surrenders some of his rights to the community.
   d. signs a contract listing the rights he will acquire.

10. According to Caesare Beccaria, the use of torture was beneficial
    a. to society as a whole.
    b. to the innocent, in certain circumstances.
    c. to the guilty, in some cases.
    d. as a means of interrogation rather than punishment.

Copyright © 1995 Houghton Mifflin Company. All rights reserved.

11. Marquis de Condorcet thought that humanity was likely to achieve
    a. very little.
    b. self-destruction.
    c. unlimited progress.
    d. the restoration of a hierarchical society.

12. For Condorcet, human beings should be guided by
    a. reason.
    b. authority.
    c. emotion.
    d. religion.

13. Enlightenment thinkers in general thought of human nature as
    a. all good.
    b. all bad.
    c. flawed.
    d. neither good nor bad.

Multiple Choice Answers

1. b	6. d	10. c
2. a	7. c	11. c
3. c	8. a	12. a
4. d	9. c	13. a
5. d		

 Copyright © 1995 Houghton Mifflin Company. All rights reserved.

CHAPTER 4

THE FRENCH REVOLUTION

Overview of the Chapter

The selections in this chapter provide a sampling of some of the evidence that has bolstered widely divergent views of the very complex phenomenon that was the French Revolution. Some historians have seen the Revolution in terms of a class struggle precipitated by the bourgeoisie's bid for power; others have seen it as an outgrowth of Enlightenment ideas, disseminated throughout French society as political propaganda. Still other analysts have emphasized the political tensions caused by the monarchy's attempts to create a centralized modern state in the context of eighteenth-century European state-building.

Value judgments on the Revolution also vary greatly. For many historians the French Revolution was definitely a good thing for the world, despite its regrettable (though peripheral) excesses. A number of recent writers, on the other hand, consider the Terror as a logical consequence of principles inherent in the revolutionary process from the beginning, and view the Revolution as the prototype of twentieth-century "totalitarian democracy," whether of the Left or of the Right. A number of recent historians have also begun to work on previously neglected topics in revolutionary history, such as popular

Copyright © 1995 Houghton Mifflin Company. All rights reserved.

counterrevolutionary activity and the effects of the Revolution on women.

The readings in this chapter should help the student understand why the French Revolution is considered one of the most controversial events in Western history.

Section 1. Abuses of the Old Regime

The selections in this section relate to some (though certainly not all) of the circumstances under which discontent became revolution. The readings also introduce some of the terminology in which that discontent was expressed.

Plight of the French Peasants includes some of Arthur Young's observations on conditions in the French countryside just before the outbreak of the Revolution. Young, a generally sympathetic observer who nevertheless found himself in some unpleasant situations as the Revolution unfolded, discusses in this selection some of the worst grievances of the French peasantry.

Grievances of the Third Estate offers a list of proposals for reform drawn up at the request of the royal government and intended for presentation at the forthcoming meeting of the Estates General. It includes some of the same issues commented on by Arthur Young.

Bourgeois Disdain for Special Privileges of the Aristocracy is drawn from Abbé Sieyès' famous pamphlet, *What Is the Third Estate?*. It includes some of the most frequently quoted (perhaps because of their brevity and pithiness) sentences to be found in revolutionary writings. As a rhetorical document it is less specific than the other two selections, but expresses attitudes common to all three.

 Copyright © 1995 Houghton Mifflin Company. All rights reserved.

Section 2. Liberty, Equality, Fraternity

This section includes only one reading, which is of fundamental significance for students of the French Revolution and its historical consequences.

The ideological importance of the *Declaration of the Rights of Man and of Citizens,* a document that was issued several times in slightly different versions, can hardly be overemphasized. Not only has it played a major role in modern French history as a "founding document" but it has served as a model for revolutionary declarations in other countries and for a mid-twentieth century "declaration" of the United Nations. It therefore deserves a very close reading and analysis.

Section 3. The Jacobin Regime

These selections illustrate aspects of Jacobin rule and express some of the thought of one of the most fascinating and controversial of revolutionary figures. One reason for the perennial fascination with Maximilien Robespierre is that he seems to some historians to represent a peculiarly modern type of political leader—one willing to destroy any number of human lives in the name of such noble abstractions as "virtue" or "the people."

The Levy in Mass gives an idea of the total mobilization of the nation undertaken by the revolutionaries.

Republic of Virtue includes some of Robespierre's most famous statements on the connection between virtue and politics. This selection also reveals the dictator's willingness to use any means to what he saw as a desirable end.

Despotism in Defense of Liberty deals with a theme common to most revolutions: the betrayal

Copyright © 1995 Houghton Mifflin Company. All rights reserved.

of the cause by "traitors" among the population. The treason in question may be imaginary, or fomented by survivors of the privileged classes, or—increasingly in revolutionary France—the resistance of ordinary people to revolutionary goals and activity. Whatever the source of disloyal behavior, Robespierre thought he knew how to deal with it.

Finally, *The Guillotine* describes the harrowing spectacle of the public executions designed to eliminate resistance to Jacobin rule.

Section 4. Napoleon: Destroyer and Preserver of the Revolution

These selections give an insight into the mind and methods of one of history's most extraordinary figures. Like Robespierre, Napoleon Bonaparte has been seen as a precursor of modern dictators.

Leader, General, Tyrant, Reformer draws on Napoleon's own words from a variety of documents to illustrate the perspective and goals of the man who played so many roles in the drama of the Revolution. The excerpt under *Leader* displays the method by which the general appealed both to his own men and to the people of the territories he occupied.

The *General* section contains selections from Napoleon's diary (which he apparently composed with a view to publication), illustrating his reflections on his own leadership and reasons for some of his successes.

Under the heading *Tyrant* there are two examples of the emperor's methods of thought control: the *Imperial Catechism*, which French schoolchildren were obliged to memorize, and Napoleon's order concerning regulation of the press.

 Copyright © 1995 Houghton Mifflin Company. All rights reserved.

The *Reformer* selection refers to the emperor's professed concern for liberal government within his empire. Napoleon, who once explained that "Constitutions should be short and obscure," writes to his brother Jerome instructing him to implement Napoleon's constitution for Westphalia because of the various benefits that this will bring to both Bonaparte and the people of the conquered state.

Questions for Discussion or Essay Assignments

1. What connection do you see between the political ideas and proposals of the Enlightenment thinkers (see Chapter 3) and the ideas of the French revolutionaries found in this chapter?

2. Make a list of what seem to you to be the four or five most deeply felt grievances expressed in the readings in Section 1.

3. Do the readings given in Section 1 offer any support for the idea that class antagonism played a role in the outbreak of the Revolution? Give examples to support your opinion.

4. Compare the American *Declaration of Independence* (in Chapter 3) with the *Declaration of the Rights of Man and of Citizens;* what are the main points of similarity and dissimilarity between the two documents?

Copyright © 1995 Houghton Mifflin Company. All rights reserved.

5. Point IV of the *Declaration of the Rights of Man* gives a definition of political liberty. Does this differ from moral liberty, or can you think of any case in which morality and political liberty, as defined here, might conflict?

6. Points III, V, and VI may be said to constitute a radical departure from earlier Western political principles. How would James I have viewed the principles stated in these points? For Volume I readers: How would Moses have viewed this?

7. Do you think that Enlightenment ideas reached their logical conclusion in the statements and actions of Maximilien Robespierre, or is his ideology a departure from Enlightenment principles?

8. Can you think of any recent political leaders who might have subscribed to Robespierre's political theories? Does he state any principles with which contemporary American politicians would agree?

9. Victor Suvorov, in his book *Inside the Aquarium* (1986), states: "Millions are killed only by those who consider themselves good. People like Robespierre do not grow out of criminals but out of the most worthy and most humane types. The guillotine was invented not by criminals but by humanists. The most monstrous crimes in the history of mankind were committed by people who did not drink vodka, did not smoke, were not

 Copyright © 1995 Houghton Mifflin Company. All rights reserved.

unfaithful to their wives and fed squirrels from the palms of their hands." (p. 62) Discuss this quotation. Is Suvorov being unfair to Robespierre?

10. The Abbé Carrichon was obviously sympathetic to the victims whose executions he observed. Do you find any statements in his account which indicate that he was trying to be objective in his description, or do you think he was distorting the scene he depicts?

11. Napoleon Bonaparte has been called one of the greatest charismatic leaders of all time. What evidence can you find in the readings in Section 4 that might explain his broad appeal? What did he seem to think was the secret of his extraordinary popularity?

12. In his letter to Fouché, Napoleon states that the "Revolution is over." Which, in your opinion, does Napoleon's reign mark: the defeat of the Revolution or its successful completion? Explain your conclusion.

13. If Volume I of *Sources of the Western Tradition* is available to students, an interesting project is to read Thucydides' account of the revolution at Corcyra (in Chapter 3) and discuss what, if any, characteristics of that event apply to the French Revolution.

Copyright © 1995 Houghton Mifflin Company. All rights reserved.

Multiple Choice Questions

1. According to Arthur Young, the French peasants suffered most from
   a. disease.
   b. high taxes and a poor legal system.
   c. civil war.
   d. the fact that they were serfs.

2. The Cahier of the Third Estate of Dourdan contains
   a. suggestions for reform.
   b. a call to revolution.
   c. a request for the maintenance of the status quo.
   d. a declaration of opposition to the king.

3. The Grievances expressed by the Cahier did not include
   a. game rights.
   b. taxes.
   c. behavior of the militia.
   d. the institution of monarchy.

4. Emmanuel Sieyès viewed the nobility as
   a. necessary to the state.
   b. partially good and useful.
   c. natural leaders.
   d. an alien and harmful group.

5. According to Sieyès, political power should be wielded by
   a. all three Estates.
   b. the king.
   c. the Third Estate.
   d. the nobles.

 Copyright © 1995 Houghton Mifflin Company. All rights reserved.

6. The *Declaration of the Rights of Man and of Citizens* states that all authority comes from
   a. nature.
   b. God.
   c. the nation.
   d. the monarch.

7. The *Levy in Mass*
   a. drafted women into the army.
   b. provided a role in the war effort for men, women, and children.
   c. was limited to professional soldiers.
   d. excluded children and the elderly from participation in the mobilization of the country.

8. Robespierre seemed to identify virtue with
   a. religion.
   b. terror.
   c. democracy.
   d. monarchy.

9. Maximilien Robespierre justified the use of terror against
   a. common criminals.
   b. the people.
   c. Englishmen.
   d. enemies of the Revolution.

10. The Abbé Carrichon thought that
    a. the executioners he observed were efficient and somewhat humane.
    b. those executed deserved no sympathy.
    c. the spectators were sympathetic to the victims.
    d. the executioners were deliberately cruel.

Copyright © 1995 Houghton Mifflin Company. All rights reserved.

11. Napoleon Bonaparte thought that leaders must appeal to their followers'
    a. imagination.
    b. reason.
    c. traditions.
    d. fears.

12. In the *Imperial Catechism,* Napoleon sought to indoctrinate schoolchildren by identifying obedience to him with
    a. reason.
    b. superstition.
    c. materialism.
    d. religious duty.

13. Napoleon supported Enlightenment ideals
    a. wholeheartedly.
    b. not at all.
    c. when they suited his purposes.
    d. when Jerome insisted.

Multiple Choice Answers

1. b
2. a
3. d
4. d
5. c
6. c
7. b
8. c
9. d
10. a
11. a
12. d
13. c

 Copyright © 1995 Houghton Mifflin Company. All rights reserved.

CHAPTER 5

THE INDUSTRIAL REVOLUTION

Overview of the Chapter

The Industrial Revolution, like the "revolutions" studied earlier in this book, is so named because of the profound changes it brought into the lives of ordinary people, whole nations, and eventually to the world. The readings in this chapter deal with important issues of nineteenth-century industrialization.

Section 1. Early Industrialization

The two selections in this section deal with the reasons why, given certain technical prerequisites in the form of newly invented machinery, industrialization and the factory system developed where and how they did.

In *Britain's Industrial Advantages and the Factory System,* Edward Baines sums up the several factors that contributed to England's early pre-eminence in machine manufacturing; he also discusses the arguments in favor of centralizing labor in the factory system.

Adam Smith's famous description of the pin-making process as an argument for factory organization of manufacturing is given in the *The Division of Labor*.

Copyright © 1995 Houghton Mifflin Company. All rights reserved.

Section 2. The Capitalist Ethic

Capitalism had many champions in the late nineteenth century because of the opportunities for social and economic advancement it seemed to offer. Making the most of such opportunities, however, required self-discipline and positive attitudes toward work, which have been variously associated with the Calvinist work ethic and with the middle class in general, although to some extent their roots extend back into Judeo-Christian culture.

Self-Help and *Thrift*, by Samuel Smiles, represent a genre of exhortative literature popular in both England and the United States. The author assumes that the basic material circumstances of a man's life are under his control, and that he can exercise that control through the virtuous behavior outlined in these selections.

Section 3. Factory Discipline

New working conditions required a type of behavior in the work place that was different in many details from work patterns in any previous age. It is difficult for twentieth-century readers to appreciate how new (and psychologically disturbing) was the need to live by the clock, to take no leisure between tasks, and to refrain from conversation and human contact with fellow workers on the job.

Factory Rules from a factory in Germany can help the reader to appreciate the new and rigid discipline imposed on human beings by industrialization.

 Copyright © 1995 Houghton Mifflin Company. All rights reserved.

Section 4. The Dark Side of Industrialization

The considerable profits to be made from manufacturing were a powerful incentive for employers to drive their workers, both human and machine, to the limits of their capacities. This situation aroused remarkably little powerful indignation for at least the first half of the nineteenth century. The medieval guilds, which in earlier times had limited working hours and provided unemployment and accident insurance, as well as other support for their members, had been destroyed. Workers thus no longer had any organization to speak for them. The religious outlook of many Protestants, which equated poverty and lack of success with sin and lack of "justification," did nothing to arouse compassion for the worker.

Report on Child Labor gives a harrowing picture of the plight of children in the early factory system.

The excerpt from Friedrich Engel's *The Condition of the Working Class in England* discusses the miserable lives and living conditions of the industrial workers.

Section 5. The New Science of Political Economy

New economic conditions gave rise to new economic theory. In the Middle Ages economic activity was regulated by Christian moral principles expressed in legislation and guild organization, but the postmedieval period gave rise to the theory of control of a nation's economy by the central government, which is called *mercantilism*. In the late eighteenth and early nineteenth centuries, economic theorists began to apply the principles of Enlightenment liberalism—understood as freedom from a given undesirable restraint—to the economy. If there

Copyright © 1995 Houghton Mifflin Company. All rights reserved.

are no restraints at all on economic life, argued the economic liberals, then natural laws (a legacy of the Scientific Revolution) will operate in the marketplace for the common good of state and people.

The Wealth of Nations by Adam Smith is one of the most influential books in economic history. This selection contains the famous passage on "the invisible hand," which would promote the common economic good independently of the intentions of individuals.

The excerpt from *On the Principle of Population* appears in some ways to contradict Enlightenment liberal principles: Thomas R. Malthus certainly denies the philosophes' premise of human perfectibility. On the other hand, since he assumes (wrongly, as it turned out) that food production could not be made to keep pace with population growth and that poverty is therefore inevitable, he gives support to the liberal concept of "laws of nature" with which the government should not interfere.

Questions for Discussion or Essay Assignments

1. In what ways could Edward Baines' description of the elements favoring industrialization in Britain be applied to nineteenth-century New England?

2. How would you characterize Samuel Smiles' view of human nature? Does it agree with that of the Enlightenment thinkers you have read?

Copyright © 1995 Houghton Mifflin Company. All rights reserved.

3. After reading Sections 3 and 4, try to imagine a day in the life of a craftsman or farmer in pre-industrial Europe and compare it with that of a factory worker in the mid-nineteenth century. Make a list of the most important differences you can think of.

4. Evaluate the concept of the "invisible hand," which for Adam Smith was supposed to regulate a free-market economy. Can you see any economic problems that could result from this doctrine? How might Smith resolve them?

5. Many historians have assumed that the general rise in the standard of living brought about by industrialism more than compensated for the social and psychological disruption it caused. Others, however, have seen in the development of modern economic organization a process of dehumanization of work and fragmentation of family and society for which material well-being is a very inadequate substitute. Develop arguments supporting one or the other of these opinions.

Multiple Choice Questions

1. According to Edward Baines, the most important prerequisites for the development of manufacturing are
   a. peaceful conditions.
   b. virtue and thrift.
   c. good laws.
   d. natural resources.

Copyright © 1995 Houghton Mifflin Company. All rights reserved.

2. Adam Smith demonstrated that dividing a process such as pin-making into many separate operations
   a. greatly increased production.
   b. slowed down pin manufacture.
   c. reduced profits.
   d. caused unemployment.

3. For Samuel Smiles, improvement of social conditions depended on
   a. government.
   b. society.
   c. the individual.
   d. benevolent organizations.

4. Judging from the factory rules given in Section 3, the factory most resembled a
   a. small family business.
   b. religious community.
   c. prison.
   d. school.

5. The Sadler Commission found the conditions of child labor to be
   a. harsh and morally corrupting.
   b. better than expected.
   c. improving.
   d. favorable.

6. According to Friedrich Engels, industrialization brought the urban working class
   a. an improved environment.
   b. a higher standard of living.
   c. unlimited opportunity.
   d. inhuman living conditions.

 Copyright © 1995 Houghton Mifflin Company. All rights reserved.

7. The readings in Sections 3 and 4 portray the lives of factory workers as characterized by
   a. self-regulation.
   b. regimentation.
   c. freedom.
   d. opportunities for creative work.

8. In *The Wealth of Nations,* Adam Smith advocated
   a. laissez-faire.
   b. mercantilism.
   c. socialism.
   d. corporatism.

9. According to Smith, the common good was best achieved by
   a. government regulation.
   b. altruism.
   c. socialism.
   d. everyone acting in his own interest.

10. Thomas Malthus disagreed with Enlightenment writers on
    a. rational analysis.
    b. the perfectibility of human society.
    c. publication of opinions.
    d. science.

11. Malthus believed that attempts to improve the condition of the poor were
    a. useless.
    b. demanded by Christian charity.
    c. the task of government.
    d. required of each individual.

Copyright © 1995 Houghton Mifflin Company. All rights reserved.

Multiple Choice Answers

1. d	5. a	9. d
2. a	6. d	10. b
3. c	7. b	11. a
4. c	8. a	

 Copyright © 1995 Houghton Mifflin Company. All rights reserved.

CHAPTER 6

ROMANTICISM, REACTION, REVOLUTION

Overview of the Chapter

The first half of the nineteenth century saw the growth of a cultural and intellectual reaction to Enlightenment rationalism, and the imposition of a counterrevolutionary political order upon a war-ravaged Europe. The readings in this chapter provide a sampling of the new romantic and conservative thinking, as well as of the liberalism and nationalism that sparked new outbreaks of revolutionary activity.

Section 1. Romanticism

The seventeenth and eighteenth centuries were a period of extreme rationalism and the cult of science. Also at that time, "classical" artistic standards of order, balance, and measure were in vogue, and precise rules were developed for music, poetry, literature, and architecture.

Romanticism was a reaction both to the overstressing by the philosophes of a narrow rationality, and to the imposition of rigid academic standards on creative artists. The new emphasis on "sensibility," emotion, and artistic freedom could produce fuzzy, sentimental writing and pseudo-Gothic architectural jumbles, but it also inspired geniuses: Haydn and Mozart were succeeded by Beethoven and Chopin.

Copyright © 1995 Houghton Mifflin Company. All rights reserved.

The selections from William Wordsworth typify some of the elements of romanticism. In his Preface to *Lyrical Ballads,* Wordsworth approvingly quotes Aristotle on poetry and contrasts the attitudes of poets and scientists to nature. In *Tables Turned,* he expresses in poetic form the sense of what nature has to teach us: not abstract laws addressed to our intellect but beauty and wisdom to touch our hearts.

Milton by William Blake expresses similar disapproval of rationalist thinkers (mentioned by name in the poem), and also expresses the anger of many of the romantics with the blasphemy and atheism of their Enlightenment predecessors.

Like Descartes, Goethe's *Faust* realizes that all his studies have left him knowing virtually nothing. Unlike Descartes, however, who thereupon retreated into his own intellect and the certainty of his "clear and distinct ideas," Faust yearns for knowledge and experience beyond that of geometric rationalism.

Section 2. Conservatism

Like artists, many statesmen and political thinkers also had serious quarrels with Enlightenment thought, especially in its revolutionary manifestations. Conservatives claimed that the philosophes, through their attachment to abstract, "rational" political theories, had failed to recognize the great importance of religion, custom, tradition, and order—both to ordinary people and to civilization itself.

Reaction to the French Revolution took shape while the upheaval was still going on, and has not yet died away. Indeed, the 1989 bicentennial of the Revolution gave rise to a passionate debate both in France (with the

 Copyright © 1995 Houghton Mifflin Company. All rights reserved.

Anti-89 movement) and elsewhere, in which all shades of opinion were represented. The French Revolution may well be one of a handful of historical events that each generation must confront and on which it must take a position.

Reflections on the Revolution in France expresses Edmund Burke's negative judgment, formed during the early days of the Revolution in 1789-1790, on the turmoil taking place in France. When this text was published in 1791, Burke could not have a perspective on the whole course of the Revolution and its consequences, but his work remains an important critique of revolutionary principles.

One of the great conservative statesmen, Klemens von Metternich, succeeded in hammering out a political settlement in 1815 that imposed stability on Europe after the revolutionary and Napoleonic wars, which had cost millions of lives. Metternich and his allies agreed to repress future revolutionary activity in the name of peace. They succeeded only imperfectly; yet, largely through their efforts, the world was spared another general European war until 1914—nearly a hundred years.

Metternich's *Confession of Political Faith* accuses the philosophes of responsibility for the death and destruction of the French Revolution. The author traces the transmission of revolutionary ideas through the middle class and discusses means of ensuring peace and order by repressing subversive activities.

Joseph de Maistre, in his *Essay on the Generative Principle of Political Constitutions,* attacks the utopianism of the philosophes and their tendency to elaborate ideal systems without reference to reality. De Maistre's disapproval of newly concocted constitutions apparently stems from his conviction that the constitution of a country

Copyright © 1995 Houghton Mifflin Company. All rights reserved.

should develop organically and include a whole complex of unwritten law.

Section 3. Liberalism

Nineteenth-century liberalism sought to maintain the principles of the Enlightenment. Benjamin Constant went further than some of the philosophes who distrusted democracy, while seeking to define its limitations in *On the Limits of Popular Sovereignty*.

Taking up the Enlightenment call for freedom in all areas of life was the influential writer John Stuart Mill. The selection from Mill's *On Liberty* gives a clear idea of the thorough-going manner in which Mill demanded freedom for its own sake, leaving out of consideration the question of whether it is rightly or wrongly exercised.

Section 4. Nationalism and Repression in Germany

If the liberal ideas on the rights of man had some influence on arousing, by extension, desires for nationalistic self-determination, romanticism had an even greater appeal for some nationalists. The romantic emphasis on emotion, tradition, history, and literature lent itself to the glorification of a national heritage.

Ernst Moritz Arndt, in *The War of Liberation*, portrays the exaltation of war in the service of the nation and the glorification of Germany and its unification as the highest aspirations of the German people.

The Call for German Unity by Heinrich von Gagern describes the nationalistic goals of the German student movement, which would be involved in the German revolutions. The emphasis is on the unification of all the German states into one nation.

 Copyright © 1995 Houghton Mifflin Company. All rights reserved.

In the face of revolutionary agitation, especially among students, Metternich and other leaders issued the *Karlsbad Decrees* in an attempt to crack down on inflammatory speeches and publications.

Section 5. The Call for Italian Unity

Like Germany, Italy was divided into many small states, some of which were ruled by foreign dynasties. The Italian unification movement contained men of many shades of opinion, one of whom was Guiseppe Mazzini, founder of Young Italy.

The excerpts from the preamble and oath taken by members of Mazzini's secret society reveal the dedication of the organization to the violent overthrow of existing governments in Italy in favor of a unified republic and to the tactics of guerrilla warfare.

Section 6. 1848: The Year of Revolutions

Although the year 1830 had seen a spate of revolutionary outbreaks throughout Europe, 1848 was to witness large-scale disturbances in almost every country. As before, France led the way during the agitation of February 1848, and later in the June Days.

The selection *The June Days* includes a speech given in January 1848 in which Alexis de Tocqueville had warned the French government of the consequences of the reigning bourgeoisie's neglect of the needs of the working class. In a later commentary, Tocqueville characterized the June uprising as an instance of class warfare, in which socialist propaganda and serious grievances of the workers were both involved.

In *Revolution Spreads to the German States* Carl Schurz gives a glimpse of the excitement generated in revolutionary circles all over

Copyright © 1995 Houghton Mifflin Company. All rights reserved.

Europe by news of the revolution of 1848 in France.

Questions for Discussion or Essay Assignments

1. List three or four points on which the romantics opposed the ideas of the Enlightenment.

2. Metternich supported the *Karlsbad Decrees* on press censorship in order to curb the spread of the ideas that led to revolution. Would John Stuart Mill have agreed? Did he think that ideas had no disruptive consequences?

3. Considering what Europe had been through during the period of the French Revolution and Napoleon, do you think that most of the ordinary people in Europe would have agreed with Metternich and Burke, or with the German and Italian nationalists? Explain.

4. Compare newspaper accounts of German sentiment for reunification during 1990 with the feelings expressed by the German nationalists in this section. Describe any similarities and differences.

5. Why do you think that the first of the revolutions of 1848 occurred in France?

Multiple Choice Questions

1. Poetry, for William Wordsworth, was a way of expressing
   a. passion.
   b. ignorance.
   c. truth.
   d. rhyme.

Copyright © 1995 Houghton Mifflin Company. All rights reserved.

2. William Blake, while defending poetic inspiration and religious faith, condemned
   a. rationalism.
   b. conservatism.
   c. Wordsworth.
   d. imagination.

3. Johann Wolfgang von Goethe's *Faust* seeks wisdom in
   a. science.
   b. the classics.
   c. the occult.
   d. reason.

4. Wordsworth, Blake, and Goethe all shared
   a. an admiration for Enlightenment thought.
   b. an enthusiasm for atheism.
   c. an interest in classical norms of composition.
   d. a romantic outlook.

5. Edmund Burke opposed the French revolutionaries because they
   a. were not radical enough.
   b. rejected the values and experience of Western civilization.
   c. were politically timid.
   d. were not English.

6. Klemens von Metternich thought that a major cause of the French Revolution was
   a. hatred of God.
   b. love of reason.
   c. popular discontent.
   d. a shortage of bread.

Copyright © 1995 Houghton Mifflin Company. All rights reserved.

7. Metternich thought that revolutionary activity
   a. was a healthy thing.
   b. should be suppressed.
   c. could do no harm.
   d. was no longer a problem.

8. Joseph de Maistre criticized the Enlightenment for its
   a. artistic standards.
   b. concern for justice.
   c. political abstraction and irreligion.
   d. scientific methods.

9. Benjamin Constant thought that the limitation of popular sovereignty was
   a. desirable but impossible.
   b. both desirable and possible.
   c. a contradiction of the rights of man.
   d. up to the king to define.

10. John Stuart Mill, writing about freedom of the press,
    a. advocated it.
    b. agreed with Metternich's view of it.
    c. ignored the question.
    d. disapproved of it.

11. For Mill, one should be free to do what one pleases unless the action
    a. offends God.
    b. harms other people.
    c. offends against standards of good taste and decency.
    d. is unpopular.

Copyright © 1995 Houghton Mifflin Company. All rights reserved.

12. For Ernst Moritz Arndt, German nationalism seemed to be
    a. a rational political goal.
    b. a peaceful intellectual movement.
    c. an irrational exaltation.
    d. an academic proposal.

13. Heinrich von Gagern wanted Germany to be politically organized as
    a. a loose confederation.
    b. eastern and western Germany.
    c. part of a multinational empire.
    d. a unified state.

14. The *Karlsbad Decrees* sought to control revolutionary activity by
    a. confiscating weapons.
    b. suppressing revolutionary societies and publications.
    c. closing churches.
    d. political reforms.

15. Giuseppe Mazzini believed in
    a. revolutionary republicanism.
    b. monarchy.
    c. peaceful reform.
    d. obedience to authority.

16. Italian and German nationalists
    a. believed in a peaceful solution to their countries' problems.
    b. wanted their countries to be divided into many small states.
    c. promoted violence to achieve unification.
    d. supported Metternich.

Copyright © 1995 Houghton Mifflin Company. All rights reserved.

17. According to Alexis de Tocqueville, the French Revolution of 1848 was caused by
    a. foreign agitators.
    b. minor political differences.
    c. social unrest.
    d. conservatives.

18. Carl Schurz and his friends thought Germany should imitate France in
    a. revolutionary terror.
    b. changing monarchs.
    c. foreign war.
    d. setting up a republic.

Multiple Choice Answers

1. c	7. b	13. d
2. a	8. c	14. b
3. c	9. b	15. a
4. d	10. a	16. c
5. b	11. b	17. c
6. a	12. c	18. d

 Copyright © 1995 Houghton Mifflin Company. All rights reserved.

CHAPTER 7

THOUGHT AND CULTURE IN AN AGE OF SCIENCE AND INDUSTRY

Overview of the Chapter

Although much of Enlightenment thought had been rejected by the mid-nineteenth century, the infatuation with science and the appeal to scientific method and scientific laws to justify new theories persisted. Determinism is the idea that all things, including the behavior of individuals and society in general, are determined by inevitable scientific laws.

This theory was proposed during the Enlightenment but did not dominate it; the most influential of the philosophes preferred to emphasize free will and rational human control of circumstances.

Determinism came into its own during the nineteenth century with the elaboration of new theories such as Marxism, Darwinism, and Freudianism. (The "isms" sometimes developed implications unintended by their original formulators.)

Section 1. Realism and Naturalism

For thinkers influenced by determinism, the highest task of the human mind was to discover and analyze the laws by which all behavior is determined. This outlook was expressed by writers in many fields.

Copyright © 1995 Houghton Mifflin Company. All rights reserved.

Vissarion Belinsky's formulation of the new artistic realism is followed by a selection from Émile Zola, *The Experimental Novel*, which shows how the positivist "scientific" approach to reality affected the arts. Zola's ideas represent a complete contrast to those of the romantic writers included in Section 1 of Chapter 6.

Perhaps the best known and best loved of the British literary realists was Charles Dickens. *Hard Times* is an example of his scathing critique of industrialism in Britain.

Section 2. Theory of Evolution

Although the idea of evolution had been discussed by several of Charles Darwin's predecessors, particularly geneticists, none had explored the subject from the same perspective or formulated it so systematically.

Natural Selection includes passages from Darwin's writings that illustrate his hypothesis that all living species, including human beings, have evolved through an inexorable natural process that allows the most fit to survive. Although Darwin himself admitted in 1863 that experimental proof of his theory was lacking, it was soon accepted as established scientific fact.

Section 3. Darwinism and Religion

Predictably, Darwin's theories aroused skepticism and outright hostility from theologians because of the apparent contradictions with Scripture. The debate continues up to the present. Like Robert Bellarmine confronted with the heliocentric theory, Catholic scholars appear willing to accept evolutionary explanations, at least in part, if the necessary fossil evidence is ever forthcoming. Some Protestant fundamentalists

 Copyright © 1995 Houghton Mifflin Company. All rights reserved.

reject any accommodation with the theory because of their insistence on literal interpretation of Scripture.

Andrew D. White describes the furor caused among Christian scholars by the first publication of Darwin's hypothesis (which White seems to treat as fact). *A History of the Warfare of Science with Theology* gives a survey of the controversy and hints at a possible compromise.

Section 4. The Socialist Revolution

Apathy on the part of governments and most institutions toward the plight of the workers aroused increasing discontent among the lower classes. Karl Marx, who ironically had little contact with workers and no experience of factory life, produced a formulation of the "natural law" of class struggle that was to inspire revolutionary activity up to the present.

The *Communist Manifesto,* by Marx and Friedrich Engels, is not only a summary of Marxist historical theory, but a catalogue of the miseries of the workers and a stirring exhortation to revolution.

Section 5. The Evolution of Liberalism

A first principle of economic liberalism had been the noninterference of the state with the workings of the "invisible hand." It soon became clear, however, at least to some observers, that a total lack of regulation meant the persistence of much social injustice and misery. An example of such injustice was the abuse of child labor, which continued in spite of mild legislative pressure against it, until salaried inspectors with coercive powers were authorized by the government to implement

Copyright © 1995 Houghton Mifflin Company. All rights reserved.

the law. The use of state legislation to remedy social ills aroused passionate debate between supporters and opponents of government action.

Thomas Hill Green makes the case for governmental action on social issues in *Liberal Legislation and Freedom of Contract*. He bases his argument on the traditional principle of the common good and challenges the liberal economists' definition of human labor as being a commodity like any other. Green's view was supported by L.T. Hobhouse in his *Justification for State Intervention*.

The opposite position, the classical liberal repudiation of state regulation, is represented here by a section of Herbert Spencer's *Man versus the State*. Spencer was concerned with the effects of unlimited state interference in economic and social affairs, and sees the question in terms of a serious threat to human freedom.

Questions for Discussion or Essay Assignments

1. How does Belinsky's concept of poetry differ from those of the romantic poets included in Chapter 6? What would you say are the two or three main points of opposition?

2. In what ways does Émile Zola express his Enlightenment principles? If, for Zola, an individual's behavior is determined by "physical and chemical" laws, how is he free to "act upon... social conditions"?

3. Do you think that a novel composed strictly according to Zola's rules would be successful as a work of art? Why, or why not?

 Copyright © 1995 Houghton Mifflin Company. All rights reserved.

4. In what ways does the work of Charles Dickens seem to agree with Belinsky's principles of realism? (If you have read any novels or stories by Dickens, have you found in them any elements of romanticism of which Belinsky would disapprove?)

5. Karl Marx claimed to be inspired by Darwin's work and wanted to dedicate a book to him. What ideas of Darwin would have appealed to Marx?

6. Compare the religious reaction to Darwin's theories summarized by Andrew D. White with Robert Bellarmine's discussion of heliocentrism in Chapter 2. What do you think Andrew White's position is? Is he a Christian? How can he reconcile the doctrine of creation with that of evolution?

7. Marx's expectation of a worldwide proletarian revolution did not materialize, although some countries did experience communist revolutions. In the light of events in Eastern Europe in the early 1990s, evaluate the practicability of the communist doctrines expounded in the *Communist Manifesto*.

8. Would Samuel Smiles (see Chapter 5) and Thomas Hill Green have agreed on the causes and solutions of the problems of the lower classes? What might be some points of agreement and disagreement?

9. Compare the remarks of Green and John Locke (see Chapter 3) on property. Do they differ significantly, incidentally, or not at all?

Copyright © 1995 Houghton Mifflin Company. All rights reserved.

10. Do you agree with Spencer that unlimited government regulation would destroy initiative and virtually enslave citizens? Can you support your opinion with examples from twentieth-century experience of socialism and communism?

Multiple Choice Questions

1. For Belinsky, the main preoccupation of the hero of realistic poetry seems to be
   a. God.
   b. himself.
   c. ideal truth and beauty.
   d. virtue.

2. Émile Zola thought that literature should be
   a. romantic.
   b. theological.
   c. nationalistic.
   d. scientific.

3. Dickens communicated his indignation at working conditions in England through
   a. vivid description.
   b. syllogistic argument.
   c. understated irony.
   d. rhymed couplets.

4. According to Charles Darwin
   a. the most fit survive.
   b. the most beautiful survive.
   c. human beings are evolving into apes.
   d. nothing has evolved.

5. For Darwin, life in nature is characterized by
   a. peaceful coexistence.
   b. the struggle for survival.
   c. stability.
   d. cooperation.

Copyright © 1995 Houghton Mifflin Company. All rights reserved.

6. Darwin thought human beings
   a. were directly created by God.
   b. are among the lower animals.
   c. evolved from lower animals.
   d. would stop evolving.

7. Andrew D. White implies that
   a. evolution is incompatible with Christianity.
   b. Darwin's theories are false.
   c. Christianity is false.
   d. the theory of evolution can be reconciled with Christianity.

8. For Marx and Engels, the key to all of history is
   a. religion.
   b. the class struggle.
   c. art.
   d. nationalism.

9. The communist attitude toward private property is that it
   a. should be protected.
   b. should be given to the workers.
   c. should be abolished.
   d. is necessary for economic progress.

10. According to the *Communist Manifesto*, the time has come for
    a. a revision of eating habits.
    b. a religious revival.
    c. free education.
    d. a proletarian revolution.

Copyright © 1995 Houghton Mifflin Company. All rights reserved.

11. For Thomas Hill Green, property and contract rights
    a. are inviolable.
    b. are limited and ordered to the common good.
    c. should be abolished.
    d. do not exist.

12. Herbert Spencer argued against social welfare legislation on the grounds that it was
    a. not extensive enough.
    b. directed at imaginary problems.
    c. a dangerous step towards socialism.
    d. not supported by enough people.

Multiple Choice Answers

1.	b	5.	b	9.	c
2.	d	6.	c	10.	d
3.	a	7.	d	11.	d
4.	a	8.	b	12.	c

Copyright © 1995 Houghton Mifflin Company. All rights reserved.

CHAPTER 8

POLITICS AND SOCIETY, 1850-1914

Overview of the Chapter

This portion of the book includes readings on a large number of sociopolitical questions that affected both eastern and western Europe in the pre-World War I era. Some of these problems remain unresolved to this day; others have recently taken on new importance in the light of recent world events. The value of capitalist ideals, women's rights, anti-Semitism, and nationalism are a few of the issues that remain relevant today.

Section 1. The Lower Classes

Despite well-meaning advice and sporadic reform movements aimed at the moral and material betterment of the poor, laissez-faire capitalism left many workers and their families in poverty and misery.

Nikolaus Osterroth's *The Yearning for Social Justice* deals with socialist organization of ill-treated workers in Germany. The Catholic church was to play a leading role in the movement for social justice, particularly after Pope Leo XIII's encyclical on the subject in 1891. Osterroth, however, describes his disillusionment with a priest who apparently sided with employers against workers, and thus influenced the author's "conversion" to socialism—a not uncommon experience among resentful workers.

Copyright © 1995 Houghton Mifflin Company. All rights reserved.

William Booth's *In Darkest England* paints a stark picture of the sufferings of the poor in the birthplace of the Industrial Revolution, while Henry Mayhew's account of prostitution in nineteenth-century London gives a harrowing view of lower-class misery.

Section 2. The Upper Classes

This pictorial essay depicts various aspects of the lives of wealthier members of society, including their dress, social life, and amusements.

Section 3. Equal Rights for Women

Women, and some men, were quick to perceive the contradictions inherent in the general approval given to the somewhat vague and undefined idea of equality in such documents as the French *Declaration of the Rights of Man* and the American *Declaration of Independence,* while at the same time at least some forms of equality were denied to whole classes and races, and to women.

Political rights for women were the original focus of most of the writers represented in this section, but other matters of concern to women emerge in several of the readings.

Mary Wollstonecraft's *Vindication of the Rights of Woman* includes a discussion of many questions concerning women beside the issue of political rights. Among other points, the author emphasizes the defects in the type of education women received in her day.

In *The Subjection of Women*, John Stuart Mill argues for legal, political, and educational equality for women, and also discusses the basic relationship between men and women. Mill seems to deny any difference in nature between men and women, and describes what amounts to a

Copyright © 1995 Houghton Mifflin Company. All rights reserved.

sinister male conspiracy to keep women in subjection.

Emmeline Pankhurst's *Why We Are Militant* also touches on the questions of legal and political rights, and includes some telling examples of lack of legal status for women in England. In addition, the author recounts the history of the suffrage movement in her country, including the considerable role she herself played in it.

Section 4. Social Reform

The readings included in this section and in Section 5 depict the considerable contrast between conditions in a western European country, Germany, and those existing in Russia at about the same time. The differences include the degree of political acumen and foresight shown by the leaders of the two countries in dealing with the needs and grievances of the workers.

Promotion of the Workers' Welfare sums up the approach of Otto von Bismarck to the use of governmental action in implementing social reform and welfare measures.

The Case for National Insurance" gives the views of David Lloyd George on similar legislation for England, partially inspired by Bismarck's reforms.

Section 5. Russia: Autocracy and Modernization

Although early twentieth-century Russia was backward and beset with serious problems that defied solution, important steps had been taken in the direction of basic reforms. The serfs had been freed in the previous century and given land; railroads had been built and economic development encouraged; and some political reforms had cautiously been attempted. Among the many obstacles to the

Copyright © 1995 Houghton Mifflin Company. All rights reserved.

success of basic reforms was the resistance to change by the various classes (including the extremely conservative peasantry), the destabilizing activities of several revolutionary and terrorist organizations, the ineffective personality of the tsar, and the baneful influence of Rasputin, who worked successfully to replace effective government officials with his incompetent friends.

A Report for Tsar Nicholas II by Sergei Witte offers a shrewd analysis of Russia's economic problems and what Witte saw as the solution.

A glimpse of the often miserable conditions in Russian factories is given in *Working Conditions for Women in the Factories*. The desperate circumstances of the women rivals, and even exceeds, the situations portrayed in the readings provided in Chapter 5, which deal with factory conditions in western Europe nearly a century earlier.

Section 6. Anti-Semitism: Regression to the Irrational

The somewhat mysterious hostility toward Jews, which has been a part of Western history since at least the Roman era, became more marked in the late nineteenth and early twentieth centuries, and took on a different character. In the past, Jews were often hated for economic and religious reasons; the new anti-Semites express their hostility in terms of race. The change in emphasis was ominous: religion and economic status can be altered; race can only be eliminated through the destruction of the individuals comprising it.

Hermann Ahlwardt's speech, *The Semitic versus the Teutonic Race,* expresses antagonism toward the Jews on racial grounds and, by implication, posits the superiority of the German race.

The passage from Édouard Drumont's *Jewish France* echoes Ahlwardt's attitude, but

 Copyright © 1995 Houghton Mifflin Company. All rights reserved.

contrasts the Jewish race with the generic "Aryans" rather than with the Germans. The language of Aryan superiority would become part of the Nazi vocabulary.

Anti-Semitism was a force in eastern as well as in western Europe, and often erupted with peculiar violence in Russia. *The Kishinev Pogrom*" describes in sickening detail the horrors of one massacre.

The excerpts from Theodor Herzl's *The Jewish State* portray the uneasiness and pessimism about the future felt by European Jews as anti-Semitism mounted. Support for Herzl's dream of a Jewish state in Palestine would lead to the creation of Israel.

Section 7. The Spirit of British Imperialism

Imperialism was part of the foreign policy of most European countries able to pursue it in the late nineteenth century, and imperial rivalries complicated international relations prior to World War I. The racism so evident in the readings found in Section 7 may be found in the writings of some of the pro-imperialists, along with other intellectual attitudes fashionable at the time.

Cecil Rhodes' *Confession of Faith* is a clear exposition of the chauvinistic idea of British superiority and an encouragement to further colonial ventures in Africa.

The British Empire: Colonial Commerce and the White Man's Burden includes extracts from speeches by Joseph Chamberlain supporting imperialism for two main reasons: it is desirable and even necessary to the economic prosperity of Britain, and it fulfills the obligation incumbent on the civilized nations to bring the benefits of civilization to savage peoples. Chamberlain stresses the benefits of British rule to the native peoples under it.

Copyright © 1995 Houghton Mifflin Company. All rights reserved.

Racism and chauvinism received reinforcement from ideas derived from the theories of Charles Darwin (see Chapter 7; readers might want to read the Darwin selection before the one by Karl Pearson given in this section). *Social Darwinism: Imperialism Justified by Nature* brings together a number of themes previously encountered in earlier readings. The racism of this selection is obvious, but here it is supported by the appeal to "natural law" in the style of the Enlightenment; "science" in this case means racial and cultural determinism—the Victorian Protestant gentleman is evolution's masterpiece.

In *British Hope for India* Lord Lytton expresses the tension between the aims of maintaining British rule while introducing liberal governmental principles to a people who had never known them.

Section 8. Anti-imperialism

The increasingly keen competition among European states for colonial territories led some thinkers to question whether imperialism was really worthwhile. *An Early Critique of Imperialism* presents the position of John Atkinson Hobson. Hobson disputes the claims of the imperialists quoted above as to the benefits of colonial expansion, and argues that, in actual practice, imperial ventures are neither profitable for the mother country nor beneficial to the natives.

Questions for Discussion or Essay Assignments

1. Compare and contrast the view of society presented by the selections from Booth and Mayhew with that given by the pictures in Section 2.

 Copyright © 1995 Houghton Mifflin Company. All rights reserved.

2. If Volume I is available, compare Mary Wollstonecraft's ideas on women's education with those of Christine de Pisan.

3. Most of the selections dealing with women's rights refer to the tyranny and injustice of men in oppressing women. Do you find any implication that women are by nature more noble and just than men and that women would create a better society if given political power? Do you agree with such a view?

4. Imagine that Witte's report was addressed not to Nicholas II but to Yeltsin. How would it apply to Russia today? What points would not apply?

5. Anti-Semitism was considered by some scholars to be completely discredited after World War II. Is there any recent evidence that the anti-Semitic readings you have read relating to Germany, France, and Russia would find support in those countries today?

6. If Cecil Rhodes and Joseph Chamberlain were living today, what opinion would they have about the situations of the former British colonies? Would they consider them to be better off or worse off than under British rule?

Copyright © 1995 Houghton Mifflin Company. All rights reserved.

Multiple Choice Questions

1. Nikolaus Osterroth changed his principles from
   a. Catholic to socialist.
   b. liberal to conservative.
   c. communist to anarchist.
   d. militant to pacifist.

2. Thomas Hill Green and William Booth agreed that the lower classes in England
   a. were prosperous and happy.
   b. needed no external help.
   c. were in desperate need of assistance.
   d. should be punished.

3. Booth, in his appraisal of slum conditions in England, appears to agree with
   a. Malthus–that nothing could or should be done to improve conditions.
   b. Spencer–that government intervention would lead to socialism.
   c. Smiles–that improvement was up to the individual.
   d. Engels–that industrialization had caused brutalization of the workers.

4. Like the Enlightenment philosophes, Mary Wollstonecraft appealed in many of her arguments to
   a. reason.
   b. custom.
   c. science.
   d. law.

5. Wollstonecraft found the women of her time to be generally
   a. superior to men.
   b. well educated.
   c. cultured.
   d. frivolous and uneducated.

Copyright © 1995 Houghton Mifflin Company. All rights reserved.

6. John Stuart Mill thought that
   a. a woman's place was in the home.
   b. women should not be educated.
   c. women should have the vote.
   d. suffragettes should be imprisoned.

7. Emmeline Pankhurst thought that women's rights might be best achieved through
   a. peaceful persuasion.
   b. violent action.
   c. the passage of time.
   d. evolution.

8. Otto von Bismarck viewed social welfare legislation for workers as
   a. unnecessary.
   b. dangerous.
   c. utopian.
   d. a Christian obligation.

9. David Lloyd George was influenced in his national insurance proposals by
   a. Herbert Spencer.
   b. Karl Marx.
   c. the example of German legislation.
   d. Malthus.

10. Sergei Witte's proposals for economic reform in Russia included all of the following *except*
    a. industrialization.
    b. business investment.
    c. low tariffs.
    d. bringing foreign capital to Russia.

Copyright © 1995 Houghton Mifflin Company. All rights reserved.

11. The condition of women in early nineteenth-century Russian factories, as described by M. I. Pokzovskaya, resembled
    a. nineteenth-century factory conditions in England.
    b. working conditions in factories today.
    c. the ideal work situation.
    d. pre-industrial farm work.

12. Hermann Ahlwardt argued against the settlement of Jews in Germany because of their
    a. control of banking.
    b. predominance in the criminal classes.
    c. hostility to the government.
    d. race.

13. Édouard Drumont believed that
    a. Jews were inferior to "Aryans."
    b. Semitic peoples had a very high culture.
    c. the Jews did not seek to dominate Europe.
    d. the French should tolerate the Jews.

14. Theodor Herzl envisaged a Jewish state that would be
    a. anti-Christian.
    b. allied with Moslem states.
    c. Asiatic.
    d. neutral.

15. The British imperialists thought that Britain had a mission to
    a. exploit primitive peoples ruthlessly.
    b. spread civilization to undeveloped lands.
    c. renounce foreign conquests.
    d. give its colonies independence.

Copyright © 1995 Houghton Mifflin Company. All rights reserved.

16. Anti-imperialists argued that imperialism
    a. was an economic success.
    b. was morally justifiable.
    c. should be pursued more vigorously.
    d. was neither profitable nor beneficial.

Multiple Choice Answers

1.	a	7.	b	12.	d
2.	c	8.	d	13.	a
3.	d	9.	c	14.	d
4.	a	10.	c	15.	b
5.	d	11.	a	16.	d
6.	c				

Copyright © 1995 Houghton Mifflin Company. All rights reserved.

CHAPTER 9

MODERN CONSCIOUSNESS: NEW VIEWS OF NATURE, HUMAN NATURE, AND THE ARTS

Overview of the Chapter

In the late nineteenth and earlier twentieth centuries, reaction against the extreme rationalism of Enlightenment thought led to increasing emphasis on the irrational. This trend became evident in science, literature, art, and modern thought in general.

Section 1. The Futility of Reason and the Power of the Will

As Enlightenment rationalism had been followed by romantic reaction, nineteenth-century positivism aroused a reaction from writers who objected to what they considered its narrow concept of human nature.

Notes from the Underground is an early short novel important for an understanding of Fyodor Dostoyevsky's later work and thought. It reflects more than the author's dissatisfaction with rationalism and his concern for individual free will; strains of thought that were common in Russian writing of the time appear in the work. Russian thinkers tended to see mysterious depths and contradictions in human nature that did not fit into scientific categories nor jibe with the optimism of the positivists. Although it is not evident from this reading. Dostoyevsky's ideas were also rooted in a

Copyright © 1995 Houghton Mifflin Company. All rights reserved.

deeply felt Russian style of mystical Christianity, which was to make him a major figure in Russian religious thought.

Section 2. The Overman and the Will to Power

The emphasis on will and self-assertion found in the Dostoyevsky selection appears in somewhat different form in the writing of Friedrich Nietzsche. Despising religion, rationalism, the common man and "bourgeois" values, Nietzsche created powerful diatribes against them all.

The excerpts given in this section from a number of Nietzsche's works illustrate his exaltation of the irrational and his admiration for the "higher" man of great force and power—the "type of human being one ought to *breed*." Many of the ideas expressed here were taken up by Nazi theorists who admired Nietzsche's work (it is not certain that he would have admired theirs).

Section 3. The Unconscious

The search for scientific laws that were held to determine and explain all behavior, a legacy of the Enlightenment, combined with the nineteenth-century emphasis on the role of the irrational, came together in the work of Sigmund Freud. Freud developed theories about human psychology through analyzing the workings of his own mind and applying what he found in his psychiatric practice.

Freud's theories, partially explained in the excerpts from some of his best known works, greatly reduced the role of reason in governing human behavior, and cautioned against harmful "repression" or urges, which Freud thought could cause mental illness. Freudianism has had ramifications in many areas besides psychiatry,

Copyright © 1995 Houghton Mifflin Company. All rights reserved.

even though in medicine many of its doctrines have been called into question. Freud himself applied psychoanalytic theory to history, and a small school of historians continues to pursue "psycho-history."

Section 4. Irrationalism and Social Thought

Fascination with the role of the unconscious and the irrational in human affairs was reflected in political and social analyses. Gaetano Mosca in *Ruling Elites* and Vilfredo Pareto in *Politics and the Nonrational* stressed the nonrational elements that seemed to them to support the rule of elite groups.

Gustave le Bon concentrated on mass psychology in a penetrating study that seemed to foretell one of the major themes of twentieth-century political history.

Section 5. Modern Art: Breaking with Conventional Modes of Esthetics

The artistic movement known as Modernism included a stress on the irrational and the unconscious together with an emphasis on subjectivism rather than communication in the arts: the artist was to express himself and his feelings, rather than a view of objective reality that the reader or viewer could understand.

The selections from Apollinaire, Klee, and Malevich reveal important ways in which the new art differed from that of earlier ages.

The pictures by Picasso and Kandinsky, together with the text by Picasso, illustrate major modernist works.

 Copyright © 1995 Houghton Mifflin Company. All rights reserved.

Questions for Discussion or Essay Assignments

1. What would Dostoyevsky's "Underground Man" think of the doctrine of original sin—the idea that human nature has become flawed, prone to evil, and is only incompletely under the control of reason?

2. Would Pico della Mirandola (Chapter 1) agree with any of Nietzsche's idea's on human nature and self-creation?

3. Are there any similarities between Thomas Hobbes's "state of nature" (Chapter 1) and Freud's view of human society described in Section 3?

4. Compare the readings from Mosca, Pareto, and le Bon with the selections you have read by John Stuart Mill. What are the main differences in approach? Can you think of any earlier political thinker who would have agreed with those represented in this chapter? Would Machiavelli have agreed with Pareto? Are there any concepts common to both Mosca and Marx?

5. Are there any similarities between the ideas of le Bon and Freud? On what points would they agree?

6. The emphasis on self-expression in modern art may be therapeutic for the artist, but what is its appeal for the viewer? What artistic standards, if any, can be applied to modern artistic productions?

Copyright © 1995 Houghton Mifflin Company. All rights reserved.

Multiple Choice Questions

1. In *Notes from the Underground*, Fyodor Dostoyevsky
   a. praises Enlightenment rationalism.
   b. exalts individual free will.
   c. expresses belief in human progress.
   d. espouses materialism.

2. Friedrich Nietzsche believed in
   a. gentleness and love.
   b. the emergence of a superman.
   c. Enlightenment rationalism.
   d. Christianity.

3. One of Nietzsche's key concepts was
   a. the class struggle.
   b. equal justice for all.
   c. the will to power.
   d. universal suffrage.

4. For Sigmund Freud, the unconscious existed in a state of
   a. dynamic activity.
   b. passivity.
   c. tranquillity.
   d. inactivity.

5. In presenting his theories, Freud made use of
   a. syllogisms.
   b. technical medical explanations.
   c. case histories.
   d. animal studies.

6. Freud thought that the principle motive force in history was
   a. reason.
   b. religion.
   c. the class struggle.
   d. aggression.

 Copyright © 1995 Houghton Mifflin Company. All rights reserved.

7. Freud's opinion of the prospects for the survival of civilization can be described as
   a. optimistic.
   b. pessimistic.
   c. the same as that of the Enlightenment.
   d. nonexistent.

8. Mosca and Pareto believed that human society is governed by
   a. reason.
   b. enlightened self interest.
   c. a social contract.
   d. rulers who can mobilize instincts and sentiments.

9. Gustave le Bon thought it was natural for crowds to
   a. follow a leader.
   b. form discussion groups.
   c. act rationally.
   d. respond only to economic motivation.

10. Modern artists attempted to follow
    a. classical norms.
    b. Renaissance principles.
    c. their instincts and feelings.
    d. objective rules.

Multiple Choice Answers

1. b	5. c	8. d
2. b	6. d	9. a
3. c	7. b	10. c
4. a		

Copyright © 1995 Houghton Mifflin Company. All rights reserved.

CHAPTER 10

WORLD WAR I

Overview of the Chapter

The Great War that erupted in 1914 had been brewing for nearly a hundred years in European intellectual and diplomatic circles. Nationalism, imperial rivalries, glorification of violent action in the name of a cause, and other elements already met with in earlier chapters contributed to an atmosphere in which war seemed, if not desirable, at least not unthinkable.

Section 1. Militarism

The organization of the Prussian state as a military machine had been at the heart of that country's national development since the seventeenth century. Chancellor Otto von Bismarck had not only continued the military emphasis but used war as a diplomatic tool—a means of promoting the power and prestige of the recently united German Empire.

Heinrich von Treitschke lived during the Bismarck era in Germany; in *The Greatness of War* he refers to the great and positive enthusiasm generated by the War of 1870. These brief passages echo several themes encountered in the previous chapter, such as the emphasis on will and the heroic qualities of Aryans.

Copyright © 1995 Houghton Mifflin Company. All rights reserved.

Section 2. Pan-Serbism: Nationalism and Terrorism

The "enlightened" eighteenth century had paradoxically been a period of proliferation of secret societies, many of them built around occult practices and organized for the purpose of achieving some revolutionary goal. During the nineteenth century, secret societies continued to play a role in many nationalistic revolts, such as the Decembrist uprising in Russia, the Polish revolution, and the Greek war of independence. In the early twentieth century, the Black Hand was such a society.

This selection gives an idea of the organization and operation of the society that plotted (and achieved) the assassination that triggered World War I.

Section 3. British Fear of German Power

For hundreds of years, Great Britain's chief commercial and political rival on the continent had been France (and, at times, Spain and Holland). The rise of a new Germany committed to imperialism, militarism, and a strong navy aroused concern in the British government.

Eyre Crowe's *Germany's Yearning for Expansion and Power* presents an astute analysis of German historical development and the mentality prevalent in influential German circles. Much of Crowe's assessment applies equally well to Hitler's Germany on the eve of World War II.

Section 4. War as Celebration: The Mood in European Capitals

Nationalism had become almost a substitute for religion, marshaling minds, wills, and emotions in the service of national glory. The cult of heroic sentiment, rather than reason, added to

Copyright © 1995 Houghton Mifflin Company. All rights reserved.

the enthusiasm that greeted the outbreak of war.

Paris, "That Fabulous Day" describes the euphoria of Parisians at the beginning of the war—an exhilaration that harks back, through the words of the Marseillaise, to the mobilizations of the French Revolution.

Stefan Zweig describes a similar scene in Vienna and adds a penetrating analysis of why his countrymen found the prospect of war so appealing.

From Berlin, Philipp Scheidemann reports the same enthusiasm among the Germans, and mentions some writings that he considers influential in shaping the mood of the people.

Bertrand Russell, a pacificist, recounts with abhorrence the emergence of war fever in England.

Section 5. Trench Warfare

No one expected the full horror of the new style of warfare: the slaughter of cavalry troops charging machine guns; the years of trench combat; the sacrifice of hundreds of thousands of lives in return for the (often temporary) conquest of a few miles of land.

The reading from Erich Maria Remarque's famous novel *All Quiet on the Western Front* describes in harrowing detail the daily lives of soldiers in the trenches.

Section 6. Women at War

The departure of men for the war brought women into the domestic work force throughout Europe. Their work was looked upon as a patriotic duty in wartime, though it also had political, social, and economic repercussions in the postwar period.

In *Genteel Women in the Factories,* Naomi Loughnan depicts not only the nature of her

 Copyright © 1995 Houghton Mifflin Company. All rights reserved.

wartime job but the manner in which it helped to broaden her outlook on many things, including the condition of the lower classes of London.

Leon Abensoir tells the story of a French woman who took over a bakery when her husband went to war, while *Russian Women in Combat* recounts the adventures of female soldiers in the Russian army.

Section 7. The Paris Peace Conference

The peace settlement of 1919 is considered by many historians to be a major cause of World War II. The extremely harsh terms imposed on Germany (in contrast to the prudent treatment of France by Metternich and his associates in 1815) left Germany in a condition of economic instability and festering resentment that Hitler would later exploit. Wilson's cavalier redrawing of the map of Europe left a power vacuum where the Austro-Hungarian Empire had been and gave rise to new grievances in such countries as Hungary, which lost two thirds of its territory in the settlement.

The Idealistic View is an apt title for the collection of quotations from Wilson's speeches given in this reading. Wilson was not only an idealist in the sense of one having lofty principles, but professed an Enlightenment style of philosophical idealism that sought to impose a rational liberal settlement on Europe, often with little regard for actual circumstances or historical background. The president's liberal bias even caused him to reject discussion of peace terms with Charles I of Austria on the grounds that the emperor had not been elected.

Point XIV refers to Wilson's League of Nations project, on which he expended enormous effort, although to his great disappointment he

Copyright © 1995 Houghton Mifflin Company. All rights reserved.

was never able to secure United States participation in it. Wilson expresses his desire to be just to Germany; he disapproved of the excessive and vengeful terms proposed by other Allies' representatives, but was persuaded to withdraw his objections in return for support for the League of Nations.

Georges Clemenceau's *French Demands for Security and Revenge* gives a good idea of the hostility aroused in France against Germany. The selection is a devastating attack on the German character and culture, punctuated with mordant wit and quotations from German authors.

Section 8. The War and European Consciousness

These selections, by writers from various parts of Europe, deal with the intellectual and emotional aftermath of the war. The clash between prewar enthusiasm and optimism and the devastating reality of the war years led to a disorientation and pessimism in the postwar period.

Disillusionment by Paul Valéry reflects the loss of optimism about human progress, and its replacement by a sense of the mortality of European civilization combined with fears for the future.

Erich Maria Remarque's *The Lost Generation* expresses the disorientation of wounded soldiers and their disenchantment with their society.

In *Brutalization of the Individual*, Ernst von Salomon argues that the soldier is set apart from the rest of society by his experiences. War becomes his life and his world, and he is discontent outside that world. There is an implicit glorification of the world of war that perhaps expresses a perennial human fascination not limited to Germany.

Paintings by two German artists express some of the anguish and horror of the war, while the

 Copyright © 1995 Houghton Mifflin Company. All rights reserved.

excerpts from Sigmund Freud's writings sum up attitudes expressed in earlier selections in this chapter: the prewar mood of optimism and euphoria about the war, the contact with the hideous reality, disillusionment, and the loss of a common cultural heritage that had formerly given a sense of unity to the citizens of European nations.

Questions for Discussion or Essay Assignments

1. Some of the authors read in Chapters 8 and 9 have agreed with von Treitschke's views given in Section 1 of this chapter. Identify the phrases that resemble expressions found in the readings from Nietzsche (in Chapter 9) and Drumont (in Chapter 8).

2. Some British (and French) writers concerned about the consequences of German reunification, have recently expressed opinions similar to some of Eyre Crowe's points. Do you think that any of his analysis has current relevance, or is it no longer applicable to today's world? Explain.

3. After reading the selection from Sigmund Freud's *Civilization and Its Discontents* in Chapter 9, how do you think he would have interpreted the general enthusiasm for war in 1914? How would Gustave le Bon have viewed war fever?

4. Evaluate the French position on the Versailles Treaty. What were the main grievances of France against Germany?

Copyright © 1995 Houghton Mifflin Company. All rights reserved.

5. What were the main causes for postwar disillusionment expressed by the readings in the last section?

Multiple Choice Questions

1. Heinrich von Treitschke saw war as promoting
   a. individualism.
   b. rational thought.
   c. feelings of unity and exaltation.
   d. lasting peace.

2. The Black Hand may be described as a
   a. Serbian debating society.
   b. pacifist organization.
   c. chess club.
   d. secret terrorist organization.

3. For members of the Black Hand, the most effective political action seemed to be
   a. parliamentary debate.
   b. public meetings.
   c. printed propaganda.
   d. terrorism.

4. Eyre Crowe's apprehensions concerning German ambitions were based on
   a. German history and contemporary German statements.
   b. French propaganda.
   c. anti-German prejudice.
   d. philosophical arguments.

5. The mood of Europe at the onset of World War I seems to have been generally
   a. hopeless.
   b. peaceful.
   c. indifferent.
   d. belligerent.

 Copyright © 1995 Houghton Mifflin Company. All rights reserved.

6. According to Roland Doregelès, Parisians at the outbreak of the war were
   a. fearful.
   b. appalled.
   c. enthusiastic.
   d. indifferent.

7. Stefan Zweig attributed Austrian enthusiasm for war to all of the following *except*
   a. ignorance of actual warfare.
   b. escapism.
   c. rationality.
   d. mass psychology.

8. Philipp Scheidemann describes the belief of German politicians that
   a. war is a political necessity for a great power.
   b. the peace of Europe should be preserved at all costs.
   c. Germany was not ready for war.
   d. war would be a disaster for Germany.

9. World War I proved to be
   a. as glorious as people had hoped.
   b. longer and more horrible than expected.
   c. shorter than planned.
   d. easy to win.

10. For Erich Maria Remarque, the war in the trenches was
   a. an ennobling experience.
   b. brutal and dehumanizing.
   c. worthwhile.
   d. glorious.

Copyright © 1995 Houghton Mifflin Company. All rights reserved.

11. Naomi Loughnan found that factory work
    a. expanded her intellectual horizon.
    b. was beneath her dignity.
    c. should not be required of women.
    d. was boring.

12. Russian women during the war
    a. avoided helping the war effort.
    b. were all pacifists.
    c. sometimes served as soldiers.
    d. were largely pro-German.

13. Woodrow Wilson's speeches and proposals reflected
    a. a sense of political and historical realities.
    b. Enlightenment principles.
    c. an understanding of non-democratic European governmental traditions.
    d. an appreciation of the importance of religious and cultural traditions.

14. Georges Clemenceau thought that Germany was
    a. a good neighbor for France.
    b. responsible for the war and still dangerous.
    c. no longer a threat to peace.
    d. the most civilized nation in Europe.

15. The mood of Europe after World War I was characterized by
    a. pessimism and anxiety.
    b. optimism.
    c. hope for the future.
    d. frivolity.

 Copyright © 1995 Houghton Mifflin Company. All rights reserved.

16. Paul Valéry expressed the postwar anxiety of European intellectuals about the
    a. lack of prospects for a new war.
    b. decline of nationalism.
    c. economic depression.
    d. possible destruction of European civilization.

17. Erich Maria Remarque's *The Lost Generation* depicts wounded soldiers in a hospital as
    a. making plans for peacetime careers.
    b. reliving glorious exploits.
    c. apathetic and disillusioned.
    d. hopeful.

18. Ernst von Salomon describes returning soldiers as
    a. set apart from the rest of society by their experiences.
    b. indistinguishable from other men.
    c. anxious to return to peacetime jobs.
    d. potential criminals.

19. In *A Legacy of Embitterment* Sigmund Freud mourned the
    a. defeat of Germany.
    b. loss of the sense of a common European homeland.
    c. loss of his medical practice.
    d. end of the war.

Multiple Choice Answers

1.	c	8.	a	14.	b
2.	d	9.	b	15.	a
3.	d	10.	b	16.	d
4.	a	11.	a	17.	c
5.	d	12.	c	18.	a
6.	c	13.	b	19.	b
7.	c				

Copyright © 1995 Houghton Mifflin Company. All rights reserved.

CHAPTER 11

THE RUSSIAN REVOLUTION AND THE SOVIET UNION

Overview of the Chapter

The Russian Revolution, like the French Revolution, was a cataclysm that changed the face of the world. Some of the basic problems of the Russian state have been touched on in earlier chapters. In this one, the focus is on the establishment of a communist dictatorship in Russia beginning in 1917, the terror and hardships imposed on its people, and their resistance and endurance.

Section 1. Theory and Practice of Bolshevism

Although Marxism had gained followers in Russia, where its doctrines had to compete with other forms of socialism, it required adaptation to existing circumstances in order to be put into practice. The man primarily responsible for this further elaboration of Marxist theory was Vladimir Illyich Ulyanov: Lenin.

For one of his most important writings, Lenin borrowed the title *What Is to be Done?* from an influential revolutionary novel written in 1864 by Chernyshevsky, a socialist whom Lenin admired. The concept of a trained intellectual elite that should direct and guide revolutionary activity was to become an important feature of Marxism-Leninism.

Copyright © 1995 Houghton Mifflin Company. All rights reserved.

Section 2. The Bolshevik Revolution

The communist seizure of power in Russia came at the end of several months of domestic chaos caused by the overthrow of the tsarist regime, the strain of continuing the war, and the incompetence of Kerensky's government.

The account by Sukhanov of Trotsky's mobilization of support for the Bolsheviks provides an insight into the mood of the audience and the type of appeal made by communism.

Lenin's rousing summons to action, *The Call to Power,* issued two days after Trotsky's speech, triggered the communist takeover in Petrograd and touched off civil war.

Section 3. The Revolution Denounced and Defended

The ruthlessness of the Bolsheviks drew criticism from many quarters, both inside and outside Russia. Members of all social classes were represented in the opposition.

Proclamation of the Kronstadt Rebels is a pathetically brave gesture of defiance by sailors and workers against the regime that was ultimately to crush them. "But life under the Communist dictatorship is more terrible than death...," they wrote, a sentiment to be echoed at various times by millions living throughout the communist world.

Karl Kautsky, in *Socialist Condemnation of the Bolshevik Regime,* deplores the violence of the Russian communists while continuing to support Marxism.

Leon Trotsky's response to Kautsky pours scorn upon the German writer's moderate views and openly justifies terrorist methods.

Copyright © 1995 Houghton Mifflin Company. All rights reserved.

Section 4. Modernize or Perish

The accession to power of Joseph Stalin inaugurated a new period in Soviet history. In his long period of rule, Stalin insisted relentlessly on the modernization of his backward country.

The Hard Line reflects Stalin's determination to push economic development whatever the cost. It also shows his paranoia, real or simulated, about the danger of attack from the West.

Section 5. Forced Collectivization

A cardinal principle of Marxism was, in the words of the *Communist Manifesto*, the "abolition of private property." If in the early days of the Revolution the communists had promised the peasants land, they soon began to organize personal holdings into collective farms. Under Stalin this process became a holocaust in which millions of people perished.

In *Liquidation of the Kulaks* Stalin explains his policy with chilling clarity and logic: the human obstacles in his path would simply be "eliminated."

In addition to murdering millions of kulaks, Stalin deliberately engineered a famine in the Ukraine, which took an estimated five million lives during 1932 and 1933. *Terror in the Countryside* describes the process of creating starvation in a rich agricultural area and how the perpetrators justified what they did.

Section 6. Soviet Indoctrination

Like the French revolutionaries, Soviet communist leaders tried to create a new type of human being by creating a new culture and developing a mythology and rituals to substitute for Christianity.

Copyright © 1995 Houghton Mifflin Company. All rights reserved.

The Cult of Stalin addresses the dictator as a god from whom all good things come. It may be hard for readers to believe that anyone could actually have given this address, but the next reading tries to explain how it could have happened.

Yevtushenko's *Literature as Propaganda* provides insight into the mentality that allowed the cult of Stalin to progress as far as it did.

By 1953, when Stalin died, at least one author, Vladimir Polyakov, was able to satirize the creation of "Soviet literature" in his amusing tale, *The Story of Fireman Prokhorchuk*.

Section 7. Stalin's Terror

Stalinism had become such a liability to the prestige of the Soviet government that Nikita Khrushchev initiated the first official criticism of Stalin, whom Khrushchev was careful to disassociate from the patriarchal figure of Lenin.

Khrushchev's Secret Speech of 1956 accuses Stalin of despotic behavior and illegal persecution of good communists.

Alexandr Solzhenitsyn, one of the great Russian thinkers in the tradition of Dostoyevsky and Soloviev, has become known for his incisive philosophical critiques of modern Western, as well as Soviet, society. He is best known, however, for his historical novels dealing with the communist era and for his monumental work *The Gulag Archipelago*, from which the harrowing *Forced Labor Camps* is taken.

Copyright © 1995 Houghton Mifflin Company. All rights reserved.

Questions for Discussion or Essay Assignments

1. Compare the last two sections of the *Communist Manifesto* in Chapter 7 with the arguments of Kautsky and Trotsky. Which one seems to draw the most logical conclusions from the premises stated in the *Manifesto*?

2. Compare Trotsky's justification of terrorism with that of Robespierre in Chapter 4. Are there any major differences?

3. Soviet leaders since Khrushchev have disavowed Stalinist rule as a deviation from true communism. From your reading of the selections by Marx, Lenin, and Trotsky, do you think Stalin's methods represented a repudiation or an implementation of original Marxist principles?

4. In *The Hard Line*, Stalin appeals to the emotions of his audience. What sentiments is he trying to play upon? Cite examples from the reading.

5. Khrushchev states that "Lenin used severe methods only in the most necessary cases, when the exploiting classes were still in existence...." Does this imply that such methods may still sometimes be necessary? Does Khrushchev disapprove of Stalin's "extreme methods" in themselves or only because they were used inappropriately?

Copyright © 1995 Houghton Mifflin Company. All rights reserved.

Multiple Choice Questions

1. According to Lenin, leadership of the revolution should be in the hands of the
   a. people.
   b. workers.
   c. professional revolutionary elite.
   d. peasants.

2. Leon Trotsky appealed to his listeners'
   a. emotions and material needs.
   b. philosophical principles.
   c. partisan political outlook.
   d. social aspirations.

3. The Bolsheviks believed in taking power by
   a. peaceful persuasion.
   b. free elections.
   c. violence.
   d. chance.

4. The Kronstadt Rebels faulted the Russian revolutionaries for their
   a. timidity.
   b. terrorist oppression.
   c. execution of the tsar.
   d. foreign policy.

5. Karl Kautsky attacked the Bolsheviks for being
   a. too faithful to Marx and Engels.
   b. insufficiently forceful.
   c. repressive dictators.
   d. too tolerant.

Copyright © 1995 Houghton Mifflin Company. All rights reserved.

6. In answer to Kautsky, Trotsky made the point that
   a. Kautsky was right.
   b. revolutionaries must use any means to eliminate enemies.
   c. Kautsky was too radical.
   d. the Red Terror would be moderated.

7. Joseph Stalin's character may be described as
   a. gentle.
   b. indecisive.
   c. ruthless.
   d. religious.

8. In order to set up collective farms, the Soviet government
   a. gave farmers a choice of what to do with their land.
   b. killed peasants who would not cooperate.
   c. confiscated the property of Politburo members.
   d. put the issue to a vote.

9. Lev Kopelev explained his participation in the massacre of the peasants as a result of his
   a. belief that the communist end justified any means.
   b. natural cruelty.
   c. psychological problems.
   d. hatred of peasants.

10. Soviet writers were expected to
   a. write anything they liked.
   b. be religious.
   c. promote communism.
   d. extol Western civilization.

Copyright © 1995 Houghton Mifflin Company. All rights reserved.

11. Yevgeny Yevtushenko implies that artists who supported the cult of Stalin were
    a. hypocrites.
    b. sincere.
    c. stupid.
    d. opportunistic.

12. Nikita Khrushchev blamed Stalin for
    a. using violence.
    b. not using sufficient violence.
    c. using violence inappropriately.
    d. being indecisive.

13. *The Gulag Archipelago* refers to
    a. South Sea islands.
    b. a Black Sea resort.
    c. slave labor camps.
    d. communist schools.

14. The prison-camp life described by Aleksandr Solzhenitsyn seemed intended to
    a. reform the prisoners.
    b. toughen up less fit workers.
    c. teach intellectuals how to do manual labor.
    d. degrade and destroy prisoners.

Multiple Choice Answers

1.	c	6.	b	11.	b
2.	a	7.	c	12.	c
3.	c	8.	b	13.	c
4.	b	9.	a	14.	d
5.	c	10.	c		

Copyright © 1995 Houghton Mifflin Company. All rights reserved.

CHAPTER 12

FASCISM AND WORLD WAR II

Overview of the Chapter

As the chapter introduction points out, many circumstances, some discussed at length in earlier chapters, combined to bring about a second world war. Despite the clear analysis of German goals that had been produced earlier in the century by Eyre Crowe and the trenchant commentary of Clemenceau (see Chapter 10), world leaders failed to assess Hitler as the formidable threat to peace that he was.

Section 1. Italian Fascism

The ideology that evolved in Italy, taking its name from an ancient Roman symbol of authority, appealed to many shades of opinion with its loose conglomeration of ideas and its proposed solutions to practical problems. In some ways, fascism harked back to the ideals of an older Europe in its emphasis on community and cultural unity.

Benito Mussolini's *Fascist Doctrines* includes a heroic view of war and national pride, a repudiation of the basic tenets of Marxism, and a critique of the impotence of contemporary liberal regimes either to solve their countries' problems or to keep the loyalty of their citizens.

 Copyright © 1995 Houghton Mifflin Company. All rights reserved.

Section 2. Conservative Attack on the Weimar Republic

Disappointed with the weakness of liberal government in Germany, some critics attacked it in the name of ideas that were at once more modern than liberalism—since they drew on late nineteenth- and earlier twentieth-century nationalist themes—and more ancient than German Christianity in their pagan world view.

The Cult of Blood, Soil, and Action by Friedrich Jünger attacks the ineffectiveness of liberal government and the corrosive effects of liberalism on traditional community life. The remedy, proposed in a turgid, hysterical style, lies in the glorification of heroic, irrational impulses in the cult of nationalism.

Section 3. The World-View of Nazism

Nazism brought together many elements of German thought that had appeared in the previous hundred years. Imperialism, nationalism, racism, and the appeal to will and emotion had become especially prominent in German thought before World War I. After the war, the same elements were synthesized by Adolph Hitler in his most famous work.

Mein Kampf has been called a blueprint for Hitler's career, which world leaders either did not read or did not take seriously enough to respond to the threat that it posed. Hitler plays on the old theme of Aryan superiority in pseudo-scientific language. He appeals to the ideals and dissatisfactions of the German people, as well as to their prejudices, and shows a keen instinct for arousing and manipulating public opinion.

Copyright © 1995 Houghton Mifflin Company. All rights reserved.

Section 4. The Great Depression and Hitler's Rise to Power

After a period of postwar recovery, during which it began to look as if a peaceful and prosperous Europe could become a reality, the Great Depression threw the global economy into chaos. In Germany, the resultant instability provided Hitler's great opportunity.

Heinrich Hauser's *With Germany's Unemployed* portrays the atmosphere of demoralization and loss of dignity among the jobless men dependent on public welfare.

Lilo Linke's *Mass Suggestion* gives an eyewitness account of one of Hitler's speeches at a rally, and attempts to account for its success.

Section 5. Nazism and Youth

The younger generation of Germans was moved to follow Hitler because of desperate economic conditions and also because of an intellectual background that included acquaintance with such philosophers as Nietzsche and German nationalist writers.

Alice Hamilton describes and analyzes the enthusiasm of young Germans for Hitler in *The Youth Who Are Hitler's Strength,* and depicts the penetration of Nazism into popular culture and education.

Section 6. Nazification of Culture

The Nazis, like the Soviet communist leaders, promoted a culture that stressed such themes as authoritarian rule by a heroic leader, nationalistic sentiments, and the superiority of German history and culture. Fundamental to this cultural synthesis was a racism that contrasted the noble Aryan or Nordic race with that of the despised Jews.

 Copyright © 1995 Houghton Mifflin Company. All rights reserved.

New Foundations of Racial Science by Hermann Gauch presents the Nazi racial mythology in the guise of a scientific comparison of Nordic and other races.

"Jewish Science" versus "German Science" elaborates on the racial theme by invoking the supposed contrast between German and Jewish approaches to science.

Jakob Graf's *Heredity and Racial Biology for Students* presents a series of questions designed to enforce thinking in terms of racial characteristics.

Section 7. The Anguish of the Intellectuals

Thoughtful observers of the European scene tried to grapple with the underlying factors that seemed to be pushing the world toward another devastating war. This section contains readings from writers in various parts of Europe commenting on the decline of the values, mentality, and leadership of the middle class, and the rise of new movements with different ideals.

The reading from José Ortega y Gasset's famous work, *The Revolt of the Masses,* includes his analysis of the emergence of the new phenomenon of the "mass-man."

Thomas Mann's *An Appeal to Reason* discusses the emergence of a semi-religious antagonism to reason that expressed itself in the Nazi movement.

Arthur Koestler discusses *The Appeal of Communism,*" presenting the economic and social dislocation that led to the growth of support for both Nazism and, in his case, communism.

Copyright © 1995 Houghton Mifflin Company. All rights reserved.

Section 8. The Munich Agreement

Despite Hitler's clearly stated intention of conquering neighboring territories, other nations persisted in coming to terms with him in the hope of preserving peace at almost any price.

Neville Chamberlain outlines the arguments for accommodation with Hitler in *In Defense of Appeasement*.

The opposite argument is advanced by Winston Churchill. In *A Disaster of the First Magnitude,* Churchill attacks the Munich agreement as a betrayal that would only encourage further aggression from Germany.

Section 9. Britain's Finest Hour

Unprepared for war, the countries of western Europe fell one by one under German control once the war had begun. As Great Britain faced the enemy alone, Prime Minister Winston Churchill commented on the course of the war and rallied his countrymen in a series of classic addresses.

The passages collected in *Blood, Toil, Tears, and Sweat* are among the most powerful and best known of Churchill's statements, reflecting the hope and courage he urged upon the British.

Section 10. The Indoctrination of the German Soldier: For Volk, Führer, and Fatherland

These selections illustrate the ideological conditioning of the German army. Besides the elements of patriotism and nationalism, the texts reveal the specifically Nazi themes of glorification of Hitler, racism, and the apocalyptic struggle of the German Volk.

Copyright © 1995 Houghton Mifflin Company. All rights reserved.

Section 11. Stalingrad: A Turning Point

Despite his nonaggression pact with Stalin, Hitler invaded Russia like Napoleon before him. The campaign proved to be a disaster, again like Napoleon's, with the Russians finally victorious.

Diary of a German Soldier depicts the change of mood in the German army during the battle for Stalingrad, from optimism to despair.

Section 12. The Holocaust

The Nazis practiced systematic extermination of enemies and "undesirables," whether prisoners of war, handicapped Germans, or members of "inferior" races such as Gypsies, Slavs, and particularly Jews.

Hermann Graebe describes the *Slaughter of Jews in the Ukraine,* which he witnessed.

Rudolph Hoess in *Commandant of Auschwitz* discusses the methodical organization of the executions in his death camp.

A survivor of one of the camps, Y. Pfeffer, gives an account of prisoners' lives in *Concentration Camp Life and Death*.

A German Perspective on the Holocaust presents a 1985 official German statement by the president of West Germany, Richard von Weizsäcker. While rejecting the concept of collective guilt, the president insists on the duty to remember the crimes of the past.

From the Jewish perspective, Elie Wiesel in *Reflections of a Survivor* also views guilt as applying only to individuals (and not to their descendants) and stresses the need for remembrance of the past. He also mentions the passive complicity of many Germans in their failure to help Jewish victims or to protest their treatment.

Copyright © 1995 Houghton Mifflin Company. All rights reserved.

Questions for Discussion or Essay Assignments

1. List some typical Enlightenment principles rejected by Mussolini. Which points do you think would appeal to the ordinary Italian voter of the time?

2. Friedrich Jünger appeals to "the will to power." Do you think he is referring to Nietzsche's work with that title, and would the two writers have agreed on basic principles?

3. Nazism has been called "right wing" and communism "left wing." To what do these terms refer? Apart from the use of "class enemies" in the former texts where the latter has "Jews," compare the basic goals and methods of communism and Nazism in the writings of Marx, Stalin, Trotsky, and Hitler.

4. Lilo Linke thought that Nazism should be suppressed, while her friend, Rolf, protested that such repression would be undemocratic. Metternich would have agreed with Lilo; would you? Why?

5. In twentieth-century America, the proposal has sometimes been made that political power should be exercised by young people because they are more idealistic and virtuous than their elders. How would Alice Hamilton have responded to this idea?

6. Some historians have drawn a parallel between the British abandonment of support for Czechoslovakia in 1938 and President George Bush's refusal to support Lithuanian independence in 1990. Are there any similarities between

Copyright © 1995 Houghton Mifflin Company. All rights reserved.

reasons given justifying the American president's position and Neville Chamberlain's arguments for the Munich Agreement?

7. Many of the early Russian Bolsheviks were Jews, although the Soviet regime soon developed its own brand of anti-Semitism. In the Nazi propoganda selections you have read, were the writers more concerned with criticizing communist ideology or with employing racial arguments? Give examples to support your opinion.

8. Compare the accounts of Hermann Graebe and Rudolf Hoess with that of Lev Kopelev in Chapter 11. Are there any differences between the communist and Nazi extermination campaigns?

Multiple Choice Questions

1. For Benito Mussolini, the state represented the
   a. embodiment of national aspirations and will.
   b. proletarian revolution.
   c. product of democratic process.
   d. result of a social contract.

2. Friedrich Jünger's nationalism appealed to
   a. reason and civilized values.
   b. cosmopolitanism.
   c. humanitarianism.
   d. emotion and cultural identity.

Copyright © 1995 Houghton Mifflin Company. All rights reserved.

3. In *Mein Kampf*, Adolph Hitler proposed
   a. racial toleration.
   b. international peace.
   c. the expansion of Germany.
   d. approval of the Versailles Treaty.

4. Hitler played upon German fears of the Jews as
   a. culturally superior.
   b. a threat to German moral and economic life.
   c. physically stronger.
   d. agents of Italian fascism.

5. The Great Depression of 1929 caused
   a. increased popularity of the Weimar Republic.
   b. the triumph of Bolshevism in Germany.
   c. financial opportunity for the middle class.
   d. psychological and economic dislocation.

6. Nazi ideology extolled
   a. the Jewish religion.
   b. Christianity.
   c. German supremacy.
   d. meekness and gentleness.

7. Lilo Linke's description of a Nazi rally attributes Hitler's appeal to all the following *except*
   a. rational demonstration.
   b. racism.
   c. national pride.
   d. emotion.

 Copyright © 1995 Houghton Mifflin Company. All rights reserved.

8. According to Alice Hamilton, Nazism appealed to young people in part because of their
   a. experience.
   b. good judgment.
   c. impatience and inexperience.
   d. reasonableness.

9. Hermann Gauch considered "non-Nordics" to be
   a. superior to Nordics in some things and inferior in others.
   b. equal but different.
   c. less than human.
   d. culturally similar to Nordics.

10. For Johannes Stark and Jakob Graf, individual physical and mental differences were
    a. due to education and upbringing.
    b. racially determined.
    c. related to diet.
    d. unimportant.

11. José Ortega y Gasset's "mass-man" embodies a rejection of
    a. emotion and will.
    b. conformity and ignorance.
    c. culture and critical thinking.
    d. rootlessness and barbarism.

12. Thomas Mann criticized the mentality that overemphasized
    a. religion.
    b. reason.
    c. irrationality.
    d. humanism.

Copyright © 1995 Houghton Mifflin Company. All rights reserved.

13. Arthur Koestler depicted the communist ideology as primarily a
    a. religion.
    b. political program.
    c. moral code.
    d. philosophical system.

14. For Neville Chamberlain, appeasement represented the
    a. will of the people.
    b. betrayal of Czechoslovakia.
    c. triumph of Hitler.
    d. king's wishes.

15. Winston Churchill considered the Munich Agreement to be
    a. a masterpiece of diplomacy.
    b. necessary.
    c. a disastrous and dangerous betrayal of Czechoslovakia.
    d. sure to bring peace.

16. Hermann Graebe described the Jews killed in the Ukraine as
    a. hysterical.
    b. passive.
    c. pleading for mercy.
    d. violently hostile.

17. The attitude of Rudolf Hoess while observing the executions at Auschwitz appears to have been one of
    a. horror and revulsion.
    b. rebellion against his superiors.
    c. detached observation.
    d. desire to help the victims.

 Copyright © 1995 Houghton Mifflin Company. All rights reserved.

18. Most of the victims in the German death camps were
    a. Jews.
    b. Germans.
    c. Aryans.
    d. criminals.

19. Richard von Weizsäcker explained that the Holocaust was
    a. common knowledge in Germany, but carried out secretly.
    b. unknown to most Germans.
    c. carried out publicly.
    d. a myth.

20. Elie Wiesel blamed the Germans because
    a. they were all guilty.
    b. many failed to help the Jews when they could have.
    c. guilt is hereditary.
    d. they all knew the details of the Holocaust.

Multiple Choice Answers

1.	a	8.	c	15.	c
2.	d	9.	c	16.	b
3.	c	10.	b	17.	c
4.	b	11.	c	18.	a
5.	d	12.	c	19.	a
6.	c	13.	a	20.	b
7.	a	14.	a		

Copyright © 1995 Houghton Mifflin Company. All rights reserved.

CHAPTER 13

THE WEST IN AN AGE OF GLOBALISM

Overview of the Chapter

This final group of readings touches on issues that have had a long period of historical development and still are relevant today. The Cold War and its aftermath, decolonization, and the future stability of increasingly interrelated world systems are some of the themes that appear in these selections.

Section 1. The Collapse of Communism in Eastern Europe

The readings in this section deal with the Eastern European challenge to communist rule on a number of fundamental issues. Patriotism, religion, Western political ideals, and the failure of communist economics all contributed to the resistance.

Milovan Djilas's *The New Class* is one of the first major works to analyze the emergence and character of the communist ruling class. The reading provides insight into the nature of communist tyranny, as well as a prophetic prediction of the current nationalistic agitation within the former Soviet bloc.

Czechoslovakia's Vaclav Havel depicts the effect of communist rule on his people in *The Failure of Communism*.

Copyright © 1995 Houghton Mifflin Company. All rights reserved.

Reflections on the Decline of Communism, by Zbigniew Brzezinski, analyzes the elements involved in the collapse of the communist system and prospects for the future.

Section 2. Violations of Human Rights

The twentieth century has been a period of unprecedented mass murders and persecutions. The postwar persistence of terrorism and disregard for human life has given rise to various organizations set up to fight for basic human rights.

Amnesty International's report, *Political Murder,* lists examples of human rights abuses in many parts of the world in 1992, and describes its efforts to mobilize public opinion and governmental action.

Section 3. Feminism

Out of nineteenth- and early twentieth-century movements for women's political and legal rights emerged a broader ideology known as feminism. Feminists analyze the causes for the "inferior" status of women in society and support "women's liberation" from all inequality. This stance often includes a rejection of motherhood, traditional marriage, and the idea of possible male superiority in anything, thus making feminism controversial even among women. Since there are no readings here from antifeminist women writers, it might be interesting for students so inclined to collect material on the antifeminist position for class discussion of this selection.

Simone de Beauvoir's *The Second Sex* is a wide-ranging examination of the disabilities which, the author believes, afflict women in both family and society. She also discusses the

Copyright © 1995 Houghton Mifflin Company. All rights reserved.

feminine personality traits that prevent women from being more successful.

Section 4. A Reaffirmation of Western Values

In reaction to the rejection and denigration of Western civilization by many recent writers, Jacques Ellul presents a detailed defense of what he sees as the West's unique and priceless values in *The Betrayal of the West*.

Section 5. Soaring Population and Environmental Deterioration

A growing sense of the economic, military, and environmental interconnections within the world community has led to increased concern with finding solutions to common problems.

Paul Kennedy's *Demographic Explosion* offers conjectures on population and environment in the twenty-first century.

Section 6. World Politics in the Post-Cold War Era

Far from inaugurating a new era of peace and stability as some expected, the end of the Cold War aggravated already existing tensions and produced instability in many areas.

Nationalism, Tribalism, and Ethnic Conflicts surveys some of the numerous upheavals occurring in the late twentieth century.

Michael T. Klare's *The New Challenges to Global Security* analyzes the various forces operating against stability in many parts of the world, while Craig R. Whitney discusses our devastating moral and spiritual decline in *A World Unhinged Gropes for New Rules*.

Copyright © 1995 Houghton Mifflin Company. All rights reserved.

Questions for Discussion or Essay Assignments

1. In connection with the reading from Djilas's *The New Class*, reread Lenin's argument in Chapter 11 for the building up of a communist elite to direct and control the seizure of power. Do you think there is a connection between the emergence of this elite and Djilas's self-perpetuating political bureaucracy? What would Pareto and Mosca think of Djilas's analysis?

2. Amnesty International has been accused of left-wing bias and distortion in its investigation of human rights violations. Critics also claim the organization ignores nongovernmental terrors and atrocities, such as the brutal "necklace" killings in South Africa and murders by revolutionaries elsewhere, thus giving tacit support to antigovernment violence and undermining political authority. How would officials of Amnesty answer these objections?

3. Would Simone de Beauvoir admit any natural differences between men and women that would lead logically to differing roles in society for the sexes?

4. Is Jacques Ellul a rationalist in the style of the Enlightenment philosophes? Which of his statements would support this view? Would any contradict it? Evaluate his general argument. Do you agree?

5. Some demographers such as Jacqueline Kasun and Julian Simon have taken issue with the bleak population scenario given

Copyright © 1995 Houghton Mifflin Company. All rights reserved.

by Paul Kennedy. They mention such moderating factors as the natural decline in fertility that accompanies improved nutrition, the continued decline in practices such as child marriage and polygamy, the existence of vast unpopulated areas of the globe that could support large numbers of people, and errors in calculations of natural resources and environmental damage (Population Research Institute, P.O. Box 2024, Baltimore, MD 21298). Look into both sides of this explosive question.

6. After reading the selections in Section 6, summarize the main sources of conflict and unrest in the world today. How were such conflicts resolved or controlled in the past? Consider such multi-ethnic states as the Roman Empire and Charlemagne's empire (both represented in selections in Volume I), the Austro-Hungarian Empire, and the Soviet Union.

7. Following the fall of the Roman Empire, what we have come to call "the West" was generally understood to mean Christendom: those European regions imbued with Catholic Christianity which produced much of the spiritual, political, scientific, and cultural foundation of modern Western civilization. According to Craig R. Whitney's article, the moral heritage of that exuberant, self-confident Europe is gone, and there is nothing to put in its place. How would you summarize the process by which the spiritual underpinnings of the West seem to have been destroyed?

 Copyright © 1995 Houghton Mifflin Company. All rights reserved.

Multiple Choice Questions

1. Milovan Djilas was one of the first to call attention to the emergence of
   a. a nonthreatening form of communism.
   b. the workers as the leaders of the communist countries.
   c. privatization of property in Eastern Europe.
   d. an entrenched, powerful caste of communist bureaucrats in Eastern Europe.

2. According to Vaclav Havel, one of the worst faults of the communist system is its effect on
   a. the economy.
   b. the environment.
   c. moral and intellectual life.
   d. politics.

3. Zbigniew Brzezinski attributed the decline of communism to its failure to
   a. recognize some of the basic realities of human nature.
   b. fully implement the ideas of Marx.
   c. exercise sufficient force.
   d. collectivize agriculture.

4. The report of Amnesty International gives the impression that violence and oppression throughout the world
   a. have greatly decreased.
   b. hardly exist anymore.
   c. are limited to gang warfare among criminals.
   d. show little sign of diminishing.

Copyright © 1995 Houghton Mifflin Company. All rights reserved.

5. Simone de Beauvoir thought that women often
   a. behave as independently as men.
   b. have very little trouble asserting themselves.
   c. cooperate in their own domination by men.
   d. have no need to work for more rights.

6. Jacques Ellul thought that Western civilization was
   a. uniquely valuable.
   b. irrelevant.
   c. outdated.
   d. bad for the rest of the world.

7. One of the most important global concerns today is
   a. too many trees.
   b. environmental pollution.
   c. insufficient use of agricultural chemicals.
   d. not enough automobiles in cities.

8. The collapse of communism has been followed by
   a. a new era of peace and prosperity.
   b. an increase in ethnic, political, economic, and religious tensions.
   c. the triumph of democracy in most places.
   d. the restoration of monarchical regimes.

 Copyright © 1995 Houghton Mifflin Company. All rights reserved.

9. According to Craig R. Whitney, late twentieth-century society is
   a. morally and spiritually adrift.
   b. increasingly religious.
   c. more rational and humane than earlier societies.
   d. less prone to violence than in past decades.

Multiple Choice Answers

1. d	4. d	7. b
2. c	5. c	8. b
3. a	6. a	9. a

Copyright © 1995 Houghton Mifflin Company. All rights reserved.